Praise ʄ

THE PARTY CRASHER

"*The Party Crasher* is a must-read for any and all seeking the way of Jesus amid the fractured mess we find ourselves in today. In our hyper-polarized, us-versus-them culture, the invitation to follow Jesus as an enemy-loving, fruit-of-the-Spirit-bearing, laying-down-our-lives-for-our-neighbors reconciler is the only viable path toward transcending the political divides and embodying the Christian vision of peace. I love the prayer that Josh invites us into—*God, give us soft hearts and steel spines*—in this timely and all-important book."

—JAY KIM, pastor of WestGate Church (San Jose, California) and author of *Analog Christian*

"Politics is the new religion. In the first century, no one separated politics and religion. In the twenty-first century, we assume they're divided. But they're not. Josh Butler explores the culture war as a religious war, driven by idols and ideologies, showing how kingdom-centered peacemaking could transform our tribalized moment. Full of pastoral wisdom, *The Party Crasher* points us toward a vision of public engagement that cuts across party divides and keeps Jesus's strange, beautiful vision of an enemy-loving, self-sacrificing people at the center."

—PATRICK MILLER, co-host of the *Truth Over Tribe* podcast, co-author of *Truth Over Tribe*, and pastor at The Crossing (Columbia, Missouri)

"*The Party Crasher* boldly and compassionately addresses the pain and tension political division has wreaked upon our country, churches, and interpersonal relationships. Josh casts a gripping vision of what it looks like to live with conviction in our cultural moment, by exposing the core ideologies of the political religions which call for the allegiance of our hearts, to subvert our bow and pledge loyalty to Jesus as the Ultimate King."

—BRE GOLDEN, pastor of community care
at Park Hill Church (San Diego, California)
and co-founder of Waves Ministries

"*The Party Crasher* is a clarion call for the church to be the church, not a chaplain to the empire, not a partisan puppet, but the body of Christ on earth. Josh blends practical pastoral care with theologically incisive observations that lead to deeper devotion to Jesus in an era when everything is politicized. This book is absolutely necessary reading for anyone who is trying to love God and love their neighbor in a polarized world."

—TONY SCARCELLO, author of *Regenerate: Following Jesus After Deconstruction* and pastor of Open Table Church

"We all give our allegiance to something or someone. Reaching far beyond the pithy platitudes often hurled at those on the Right or the Left, Josh pulls everyone in by acknowledging one simple truth: For many of us, our allegiance is not inherently or naturally to Christ. So how do we, with our different political leanings, come to the table of Christ and sit in unity? *The Party Crasher* serves as a guide to answering this question that all followers of Christ should wrestle with."

—BRENNA BLAIN, Bible teacher, author of *Can I Say That?*,
and host of the *Can I Say That?* podcast

"*The Party Crasher* is a gospel-centric call back to the lordship of Christ and his kingdom. With clarity, humility, and wisdom, Josh masterfully gives us the necessary tools to break free from the echo chambers that dominate the Left and the Right, providing pastoral direction out of the political and cultural polarization wreaking havoc in the church today. This is the right book for a time such as this."

—JOSH WHITE, lead pastor of Door of Hope (Portland, Oregon) and author of *Stumbling Toward Eternity*

"*The Party Crasher* confronts and exposes the idols we've too generously harbored in our hearts. It is, to be sure, a wildly uncomfortable read. In the Pentecostal movement, we call it 'having your mail read.' But goodness gracious, this book is wildly needed right now. It challenges our false religions, idolatrous ideologies, and misappropriated loves with Christ's expansive kingdom. Josh has written a book that should shape the church for years to come. Highly recommended."

—A. J. SWOBODA, PH.D., associate professor of Bible, theology, and world Christianity at Bushnell University and author of *After Doubt*

THE PARTY CRASHER

THE
PARTY
CRASHER

*How Jesus Disrupts Politics as Usual
and Redeems Our Partisan Divide*

JOSHUA RYAN BUTLER

MULTNOMAH

Details in some anecdotes and stories have been changed to protect the identities of the persons involved.

2024 Multnomah Trade Paperback Original

Published in the United States by Multnomah, an imprint of Random House, a division of Penguin Random House LLC.

MULTNOMAH is a registered trademark and the M colophon is a trademark of Penguin Random House LLC.

Trade Paperback ISBN 978-0-593-60067-2
Ebook ISBN 978-0-593-60068-9

The Library of Congress catalog record is available at
https://lccn.loc.gov/2023012275.

Printed in the United States of America on acid-free paper

waterbrookmultnomah.com

2 4 6 8 9 7 5 3 1

Most Multnomah books are available at special quantity discounts
for bulk purchase for premiums, fundraising, and corporate and educational
needs by organizations, churches, and businesses. Special books or book excerpts
also can be created to fit specific needs. For details, contact
specialmarketscms@penguinrandomhouse.com.

To Jim Mullins, one of the wisest and humblest leaders I know. The best ideas in these pages I've learned from you; many of the stories are inspired by your genius. It's been an honor to co-pastor with you. You ask insightful questions, your creative imagination is unmatched, and you are a true friend.

To Redemption Tempe, for the honor of being your pastor for five years. Your allegiance to the King as citizens of his kingdom has inspired and embodied the stories in these pages. You've modeled unity in Christ, staying at the table in the midst of polarization, and the fruit of the Spirit, throwing a better party for the world.

CONTENTS

AUTHOR'S NOTE

I wrote this book while a pastor at Redemption Tempe in Arizona. The stories herein are, in many ways, a celebration of God's work in this amazing church community that our family was honored to call home for many years. When I speak of "our church" in the pages to come, I am referring to Redemption Tempe. After the book was completed, we found ourselves returning to our hometown in the Pacific Northwest, closer to our extended family. Yet this book remains inspired by, written from within, and dedicated to the amazing followers of Jesus and the kingdom party happening at Redemption Tempe.

INTRODUCTION

The Party Crasher

Kyle wasn't invited. Back in high school, I was the awkward book nerd; he was the jock football star. I didn't even think to extend an invitation. So there was no front door thrown open, no red carpet rolled out when he arrived. I was content with the party I had, boring as it might have been. Yet he showed up anyway. At my house.

Kyle crashed my party.

He disrupted the cliques of high school politics-as-usual. Kyle refused to hang out with the usual suspects, befriending the goths and the misfits, the pretty and the put together, the artists and military brats and nerds (like me)—and yes, the athletes too. He breached social circles and broke down walls, forming a shockingly new and eclectic community.

Kyle was the life of the party. The atmosphere changed when he walked in. The laughter got louder, the stories grander, the friendships deeper. He crashed a party not to tear it down but to build it up. It wasn't the beverages he brought; it was his presence. Things got better with him around. Yet there was something else he was known for . . .

Kyle threw an even *better* party. His backyard bashes were epic. My memories are vivid: awake at 2 A.M. in the hot tub, with the firepit blazing, truly alive with close friends and never wanting to go home. Kyle drew me out of my bubble, into a wider horizon and more expansive community than I would have otherwise thought possible. Once I tasted this party, the others paled in comparison. My former bubble seemed boring and stale. I'm glad he crashed my party.

Kyle was like Jesus.

* * *

Jesus is crashing the party. Or, better yet, the parties. This is not a book about high school politics but American politics (though there are many similarities). Increasingly, many Christians feel they don't fit comfortably within either party. Each side demands ultimate allegiance to a "party package" that is incompatible—at points—with the Christian faith. As temperatures rise, the hostility and division are tearing friendships, families, and churches apart. I'll share loads of firsthand stories in the pages ahead.

The partisan boxes become like high school cliques, isolated bubbles filled with people who think alike. Sadly, the gossip, slander, and drama are worse than any locker room or hallway. The party conversation quickly becomes status seeking, scripted, and stale.

This issue is bigger than Democrat and Republican. In chapters 1–3, I'll offer fresh insight on the four distinct values driving the division today. (Surprise: There are not just two parties; there are four—and they're not that fun these days!) I have found these four values helpful to explain "What the heck just happened?" in American politics.

I call these "the four political religions." People are converting to them in droves, with zealous devotion to guarding the tenets of their newfound faith. We'll explore how politics is more religious than we often think and how the gospel is actually political—though not in the way you might expect!

Fortunately, Jesus is the Party Crasher. Like Kyle, the boundary-breaking prom king, the King of kings is calling together people who lean in different directions but refuse to bow to the partisan religions of our day. Whichever side you're on, Jesus is disrupting politics-as-usual and calling you into a bigger, bolder, grander vision that can redeem our partisan divide.

Jesus shows you how to bring his life to your party. In chapters 4–6, I'll focus on political discipleship. We'll get practical with ten political commandments for Christlike engagement. We'll learn how to be peacemakers rather than peacefakers or peacebreakers. We'll explore how to be bold and take a stand without compromising the fruit of his Spirit. Jesus shows you how to be actively engaged in politics without destroying your soul.

I'm not here to tell you to leave your party and stop caring about politics. Actually, it's the opposite. I want to encourage you to be a better disciple of Jesus in whichever party or place you're in—one who makes it better because of your presence there. I do want to show you how to resist the idols in your circles (every party has them), but I hope you'll finish this book caring *more* about the public life of God's world and feeling equipped to go about it in a way that's faithful to the King of heaven and earth.

I'm also not here to tell you how to vote. I'm a pastor, not a pundit. But if I'm a good pastor (which I try to be) and tell you there's a threat to your life with God, it's probably a good idea to listen. The reality is, people are spending billions of dollars to draw your allegiance away from Jesus and divide the body of Christ. And it's working. There are idols and ideologies offering false visions of salvation that ultimately will not satisfy. I want to inspire and equip you, in this volatile climate, to pledge your allegiance to the King of kings and live faithfully as a citizen of his kingdom.

Jesus is throwing a better party. In chapters 7–9, we'll look at how to get in on his kingdom celebration. I'll offer formational practices for a polarized world. We'll learn from ancient wisdom in the church to reimagine a better future for our children. We'll examine how the church itself *is* political and find creative options for what our public presence as citizens of the King might look like today.

I want to make you a party crasher, like Jesus, who refuses to conform to the partisan boxes and scripts of our day, in order to offer a better political vision and a more life-giving kingdom presence to the world. I'm so glad Kyle crashed my party, but I'm even more exuberant that Jesus broke through my bubble and called me into the expansive embrace of his kingdom. The King of kings is throwing a feast, and you're invited.

Join the party.

THE PARTY CRASHER

1

THE FOUR POLITICAL RELIGIONS

Half the congregation disappeared. Out of three thousand people, around fifteen hundred left—and left angry. What happened? A handful of influential members walked away and sought to take down the church on their way out. They scoured pastors' personal social media feeds, stalked the accounts of the pastors' spouses, and meticulously watched sermons, looking for any ammunition to take down the church. They started email chains with every person they knew, spreading misinformation, rumors, and slander. They made YouTube videos saying the lead pastor was under the influence of Satan. They raced to another local church and asked that church to start a sermon series attacking the place they'd left. And it worked.

The congregation split in half.

This was a church I loved that our church had partnered with, in the same city. So it hit home personally for our congregation, too. The cause for this mass exodus? Political ideology.

I'll share more of my own church's story in the pages ahead. Mistakes we've made. Things we've learned. Convictions that have grown. We took punches from both the Left and the Right, in similar measure. And I know we're not alone. Christians are facing partisan division in their families, friendships, and churches at unprecedented levels. The body of Christ is fracturing along political fault lines. Partisan politics is crashing Jesus's kingdom party. The cause?

People are converting to the political religions.

THE POLITICAL RELIGIONS

Imagine you wake up tomorrow and a third of your church has converted to another religion. Some to Buddhism, others to Islam, others to Hinduism. One dude's now a Zoroastrian.

But they're still part of your church. They proselytize fellow church members over coffee, post their favorite devotional mantras on Instagram, share videos of their favorite spiritual guru's teaching on YouTube, and debate the tenets of their newfound faith on Facebook—not seeming to recognize there's a conflict with the faith they've long professed.

Eventually, when friends refuse to join them, they break fellowship. When family members don't share their zeal, they distance themselves. They seek new communities who will worship the way they now do. Your community is fracturing, and many people are wondering how to respond. Here's the thing: This isn't fiction.

This has actually happened.

Untold numbers of Christians have recently converted to new religions. These are friends and family members within our churches, and it's happening right under our noses. It might not be a third of the church, but it's a lot. However, we haven't recognized them as conversions because they're not turning to the typical old-school world religions. They're turning to the new-school political religions.

There are four political religions that masses of people are increasingly converting to—in both our culture and our churches. I'm not calling them religions to be cute. The root of the word *religion* means something like "devotion," and there's arguably no greater zeal or devotion many people are showing today than to their political ideology and tribe.[1] I want to explore the sacred rituals of each political religion—its priests and prophets, its authoritative texts and repeated mantras, its symbolic temples, sacred cows, and purity boundaries. Each has its own inflexible set of rules and expectations and will kick you out if you break them.[2]

Each is competing for our ultimate allegiance.

These political ideologies are a primary feature of our cultural moment—in America at least, though there are similar trends throughout the West and around the world—and a central challenge for the church today. I want to explore how political rituals invest each ideology with transcendent weight and power; how they shape us with a particular story, meaning, and hope; and how they threaten to displace God as the true center of our lives.

All of them are a pale substitute for Jesus's kingdom party.

My Story

Friends and I first recognized this phenomenon in 2016. What started as good discourse between people we knew and loved began to look a lot like conversion, undertaken with religious zeal. It happened on the Left *and* on the Right. Fellow Christians began to give more attention to the words of pundits than to the words of Scripture, to break fellowship with longtime friends in the faith, to cut out family members who saw the world differently.

As pastors, we saw couples we had counseled and married,

friends we had walked and cried with through suffering or sat
with at the deathbed of a loved one, angrily break ties because
they disagreed with a fellow church member.

This was more than classic political debate. These disagreements possessed, for those involved, transcendent purpose. We
witnessed intense evangelism from Twitter to TikTok proclaiming the good news of their political saviors. We saw new forms of
catechesis, with sacred texts on Fox and CNN, with rising gurus
on YouTube educating adherents on the doctrines of the faithful.
Each side cultivated sacred boundaries to divide the pure from
the impure, the faithful and orthodox from the heretics.

It made us realize that the religions of our day are political
and cultural ideologies. No one I know is converting to Buddhism or Islam. But loads of people are giving their deepest allegiance to political ideologies competing with their allegiance
to Christ, the King of kings. Many people are converting without even knowing it—they don't recognize the religious nature
of their newfound ideologies. They seem oblivious that it's
crashing their allegiance to Jesus.

In this chapter, I want to describe these ideologies in religious
terms to illuminate the nature of their appeal and the temptations they pose. A good place to start is the Four Americas.

The Four Americas

We tend to talk about politics as Left and Right, but this doesn't
do justice to the current landscape, which is more fractured and
complex. In *The Atlantic,* George Packer wrote a fascinating
cover story on "The Four Americas," and it has since become an
influential book.[3] He observed four different cultural narratives—
different "Americas"—that are significantly shaping our politics.

- **Smart America:** the worldview of Silicon Valley and the professional elite, who believe we can use science, technology, and strong institutions to change the world.

- **Free America:** the worldview of the suburbs, with an emphasis on free markets and hard work, dedicated to caring for whatever small patch of the world we're on and contributing to a thriving economy.

- **Just America:** the worldview of the urban core, with an emphasis on citizens as members of identity groups that inflict or suffer oppression, with a call to dismantle unjust systems.

- **Real America:** the worldview of the Midwest and rural areas, with an emphasis on loyalty to deep roots and protection from outside threats.[4]

Keep in mind that Packer is not saying the fourth group is more "real" than the others; he's simply identifying the quadrants with language popularly used for them. Also, there's complexity and nuance in the details of these four Americas, broad brushstrokes and all, but I think we get the picture.

When I first read Packer's article, my immediate response was, *He stole that from my friend Jim!* (I'm joking, of course. I doubt he has heard Jim's sermons.) Jim and I were co-pastors, and he's been talking about this idea for years. Jim and I used similar categories to help our church navigate the choppy waters of past election seasons.[5]

Jim uses different terms to describe the Four Americas, which I find more helpful. While Packer's language helps to recognize these movements in popular culture (on a *sociological* level), Jim's language helps to understand the values and ideological roots

driving these movements and engage them biblically (on a *theological* level).

Jim's terms are illustrated in the following diagram, which
we'll be using throughout this book. The key words in each
quadrant speak to a core value at the heart of its ideology.

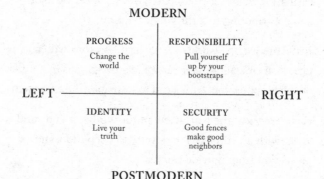

- **Progress** (versus "smart"): to speak to the upper left's strong
  belief in the value of science, technology, and institutions to
  change the world for the better.

- **Responsibility** (versus "free"): to speak to the upper right's
  strong belief in hard work, family values, and personal
  ownership to build flourishing communities.

- **Identity** (versus "just"): to speak to the lower left's strong
  belief in self-expression, anti-discrimination, and a
  recognition of others' unique stories to tackle oppressive
  legacies and build a more just society.

- **Security** (versus "real"): to speak to the lower right's strong
  belief in loyalty, local identity, and protection from external
  threats to establish the conditions for a thriving community.

It's worth observing that all four of these values are good in their proper place, with something to bring to the table. (More on that in chapter 2.) What if we approached our political "opponents" with the assumption that they have something good to contribute? That there's something to learn from their perspectives? How might that help our discussions be less heated and more productive? Yet each value can also become distorted when made ultimate and uprooted from God's creational design.

You'll also notice there is a "top-down" axis on this diagram, not just the typical Left-Right axis. This represents *modernity* and *postmodernity*. I will make the case (following my friend Jim) that this is the underlying current that has "split" the Left and Right sides of the traditional political spectrum and helps explain why some of the deepest conflicts today are not simply between Left *versus* Right but between different camps *within* the Left and the Right. (More on that in a minute.) Postmodernity has crashed the traditional political parties.

For now, let's explore each of these four quadrants as religions, identifying their creeds and core doctrines, their high priests and sacred texts, their temples, boundaries of purity, and formational practices. An important caveat: My goal in this chapter is simply to *describe* these quadrants, not place judgment on them. (So no need to get defensive if the quadrant you most identify with comes up!) In future chapters, we'll seek to *prescribe* the kingdom; here we're simply seeking to get the lay of the land.

THE RELIGION OF PROGRESS

The Religion of Progress, in the upper-left corner, lives by the creed "We can change the world." This is an optimistic religion that believes salvation comes through scientific discovery, human ingenuity, and technological advancement. It places faith in advanced education, strong institutions, thorough research, and robust public policy.

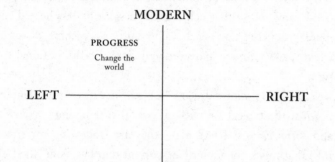

This religion thrives in what Packer calls "Smart America": Think Silicon Valley, Google and Facebook, Steve Jobs and Bill Gates, the smartphone and the tech boom, artificial intelligence and medical breakthroughs. Its location in the upper half of the diagram means it is *modern* (rather than *postmodern*), reflecting a strong belief in science, technology, and institutions. Believers here place a devout faith in these things to achieve *progress*, building a more just, beautiful, and thriving world.

This religion's high priests have been people like Bill Gates, the Clintons, and Steve Jobs, rallying the faithful toward progress and forming foundations to mediate its transcendent truths. Its most renowned worship leader is Bono, singing hymns to unite and uplift humanity around ending global poverty, AIDS, and hunger. Steven Pinker and Sam Harris are leading apologists for the power of its gospel, defending the modern ascendance of our civilization through science and reason to unprecedented heights while calling us to leave behind the super-stitions of the past.

This religion's sacred texts are found in places like CNN, *The New York Times,* NPR, and—for its more radical fundamentalists —Mother Jones. TED Talks are its sermons and academic re-search its scripture, where the devout turn for truth and holy instruction.

The university is its temple, particularly the STEM depart-ment, where you can ascend the ranks of the saints with a de-gree, which empowers you to work wonders that miraculously transform the world.

Zealous laity can be found waiting eight hours in line at the Apple store to enter its sanctuary, bestow an offering, and receive from an acolyte its latest blessing to the faithful: the iPhone.[6] This iconic relic's updated version (to be kept on your person like an amulet at all times) will allow you to approach transcendence, moving closer to *omniscience* (knowing everything that's happen-ing in the world), *omnipresence* (staying connected to friends, fam-ily, and even strangers thousands of miles away), and *omnipotence* (with the power of the universe in the palm of your hand).

THE RELIGION OF RESPONSIBILITY

The Religion of Responsibility, in the upper-right corner, lives by the creed "Pull yourself up by your bootstraps." This is also an optimistic religion, but its faith is centered on the power of per-sonal potential. It preaches the gospel that the world will be saved through hard work, good moral values, and people who are responsible for their family and their property. It places faith in the free market, business entrepreneurship, and individual liberty.

MODERN

PROGRESS   RESPONSIBILITY

Change the   Pull yourself
world   up by your
                        bootstraps

LEFT ——————————————|—————————————— RIGHT

POSTMODERN

This religion thrives in what Packer calls "Free America": Think the suburbs, Wall Street and Ronald Reagan, classic conservatism and the free market, family values and strong businesses, hard work and personal responsibility.

In the upper-right quadrant, this religion shares with the upper-left a modern belief in reason, an objective order to the world, and legitimate moral authority to enforce a more just society. Its believers also share a faith in strong institutions, though the emphasis here is on business and family, rather than government. Business is the economic engine to drive society forward, with owners at the wheel and responsible workers pushing the gas pedal rather than bureaucratic intervention siphoning off the fuel and slamming on the brakes. When it comes to government, the emphasis is on *limited* rather than *expansive*, to avoid interference with the power of the market.

Historically, Ronald Reagan was the iconic high priest of this quadrant ("Man is not free unless government is limited"),[7] with Milton Friedman its strongest economic apologist and Newt Gingrich its public herald. Today, public figures have arisen to take the baton, like Jordan Peterson shepherding his online megachurch with the philosophy of Admiral William McRaven

("If you want to change the world, start off by making your bed"[8]); Ben Shapiro exhorting his congregation while publicly defending the faith; Jocko Willink guiding novices into the monastic order of extreme ownership; and the *Dirty Jobs* guy, Mike Rowe, modeling the virtues of hard work as a path to sanctification.

The sacred texts for this religion are found in places like Fox News, *The Wall Street Journal,* and the Daily Wire. Its holy scripture is the stock market, updated for hourly observances of meditation. Those seeking to advance in its doctrines can find deeper instruction in think pieces at *National Review* and *The Federalist.* Scholastics wishing to develop new resources for catechesis are invited to apply to the Heritage Foundation or the American Conservative Union. Thought leaders can be found at the annual denominational CPAC assembly.

If the temple for *progress* was the university, the temple for *responsibility* is the home with a white picket fence and two-car garage, a reward bestowed upon the faithful as a sign of divine approval, where hard work receives its recompense, family values can be lived out, and the individual may recharge from their responsible contribution to the world.

Now, before we shift to the lower quadrants, we need to describe modernity and postmodernity to understand what's driving the shift.

MODERNITY AND POSTMODERNITY

Modernity and postmodernity are big concepts. If you're a philosophy major, you'll probably want to slap me for how simplistic I'm about to be. But I'll take your slap over having all the other readers falling asleep.

Modernity, if I can offer a visual stereotype, is the scientist in a lab coat with a microscope, dissecting and studying the world. It's a worldview that grows out of the Enlightenment, with a faith in reason, the scientific method, and building strong institutions that will solve the world's problems. It's a very optimistic outlook that says we need to use the rational aspects of our minds to study the world and invent solutions to improve it.

Postmodernity is a reactionary movement focused on deconstructing the ideas and institutions of modernity. It grows out of seeing some of modernity's failures: world wars, nuclear weapons, and evil things like eugenics done in the name of science and progress. In the words of Jean-François Lyotard (what a cool name!), postmodernity is "incredulity towards metanarratives."[9] In other words, it says, *Don't believe in big stories, big universals.* Rather, your understanding of reality and truth should come from within, from the self, from your unique story as an individual. Anything larger is just trying to limit and oppress people.

Postmodernity, to offer another visual stereotype, is an artist painting a picture of (*drumroll . . .*) the artist. He's creatively expressing himself. If modernity is about discovering and defining the world, postmodernity is about constructing and creating one's own world.

While the upper-left and upper-right quadrants have been shaped by modernity, the lower-left and lower-right quadrants have been shaped by postmodernity. As previously mentioned, all four quadrants offer good insights and contributions, yet each one has an idol that's trying to replace God. Each has a functional religion that emerges and competes with our allegiance to Jesus, seeking to crash our faith.

Let's now move to the lower quadrants.

THE RELIGION OF IDENTITY

The Religion of Identity, in the lower-left quadrant, has a creed of "Live your truth." Don't let anyone else tell you how to live *your* life. You are the one who crafts your identity. Rather than universal truths or morality, the focus is on discovering, cultivating, and constructing oneself.

This religion thrives in what Packer calls "Just America": Think the urban core, Ta-Nehisi Coates and Elliot Page, San Francisco and Boston, race and gender placards, protests against a legacy of injustice, and Tik Tok and Instagram posts with an ethos of personal self-expression, dismantling oppression, and experiencing the world.

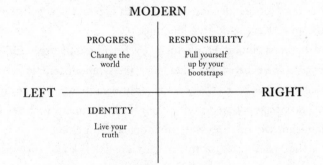

MODERN

PROGRESS   RESPONSIBILITY
Change the   Pull yourself
world   up by your
                   bootstraps

LEFT ——————————————————————— RIGHT

IDENTITY
Live your
truth

POSTMODERN

As a lower quadrant, this religion is pessimistic toward the ideas and institutions of modernity, observing how they have historically been used to oppress people and have manipulated language to justify their injustice. Although there is still a desire for progress, this distrust in the external pushes the vehicle for transformation within. The locus of faith is no longer "out there" in science, technology, and strong institutions but rather "in here," discovering and expressing one's most authentic desires—

being oneself—and freeing up others to do the same. The objective is traded for the subjective.

This religion is not completely relativistic, because it also has a big moral push that says that any ideas or institutions that get in the way of self-expression must be dismantled and deconstructed.

The preachers of this religion are pop-culture icons like Lady Gaga and Lil Nas X, modeling the way of salvation through performative self-expression and continual reinvention. Its prophets are political leaders like Alexandria Ocasio-Cortez, proclaiming a gospel that the world will be saved through deconstructing and dismantling all institutional roadblocks that keep people from their authentic selves. This religion's most rampant conversion growth has been seen on the front lines of the race and gender revolutions, with big-tent evangelists like Ibram X. Kendi and Jazz Jennings.

If the symbolic temple for *progress* is the university, and for *responsibility* the white picket fence, the symbolic temple for this religion is the protest: where the faithful gather to sing the choir of the vox populi, registering their disillusionment with the establishment and expressing their demand for change.

The sacred texts for this religion are TikTok and Instagram, where influencers provide a menu of available options for constructing one's own personal identity and customized brand. Try them on and, if you like something, make an offering to the building campaign. (For example, "Share this post" to support the construction of this influencer's online cathedral.)

Catechism in this religion is provided through the Disney script, where youngsters learn that family, tradition, and authority are obstacles to be overcome in their project of self-realization. Elsa learns to "let it go," Luca leaps out of the water, and Moana sets out on her own until she is able to declare, "I am Moana!"

Each must look within to discover their truest self and guiding light, over and against the external sources that lay a claim upon their existence. Granted, I love watching these films with my children, and there's certainly something of the classic "hero's journey" here as well. Yet themes from the postmodern cult of identity are also clearly at play, especially when compared with classic films and children's tales.

Those in this religion are tempted to quickly swap out career choices, hobbies, and spouses when they no longer serve the higher purpose of a vehicle for the construction of identity.

Personality tests like the Enneagram are rites of passage to this sacred order, providing you with a language to discover and share the unique strengths and temptations that make you *you*. (It's funny, I've gotten more hate mail when I say anything less than enthusiastically positive about the Enneagram than when I do the same about most any other topic.) I'm not saying such personality tests are bad—they can be useful—but simply that their skyrocketing popularity today is iconic of the identity quadrant in our cultural moment. (Discover and cultivate the truest you!)

Adherents of this religion frequently claim to resist consumerism ("the sins of their fathers") and prefer minimalism. Yet this practice is deceptive—it is simply a new *type* of consumerism. We consume experiences. We want the awesome meals at the hot new restaurants, the killer vacations in amazing locations, the craft coffee, local microbrew, latest Broadway hits, and prestigious music festivals. And, of course, we want to document the whole thing on social media along the way.

Many have called this "the experience economy." We've gone from *buying* things to *doing* things. A sign of status used to be the logo on your jacket or handbag; today, it's the location of your latest Instagram post. Honest confession: My wife and I used to brag, "We're not into stuff; we're into experiences" (thinking that made us less consumerist). But now we've realized, *That's just a new form of consumerism!* It's centered on the god of "me," on the pilgrimage to cultivate the sacred identity of the self.

THE RELIGION OF SECURITY

Finally, the Religion of Security, in the lower-right quadrant, lives by the creed "Good fences make good neighbors." We live in a dangerous world. Security allows us to prosper as individuals, families, and local communities. We need boundaries and borders to keep people safe. Insiders share codes of conduct, or rules of behavior, for how we live together. We should display thick bonds of loyalty to insiders and be wary of how outsiders can threaten our way of life.

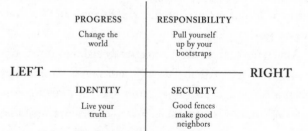

This religion thrives in what Packer calls "Real America": Think the heartland left behind by the coastal economic boom, Sarah Palin and Tucker Carlson, hometown identity and jobs shipped overseas, Detroit and the decline of manufacturing, Appalachia and the epidemic of meth addiction and unemployment.

As a lower quadrant, this religion is pessimistic toward the institutions of modernity. The deep-state government wants to take away your rights. Big Pharma medicine is pushing its pills and vaccines. The "fake news" mainstream media is deceiving you. The elites are out to get you, using language games to oppress you. The faithful need to fight against those things.

Unlike its postmodern counterpart in the left quadrant, the concern here is not that institutions are limiting your self-expression so much as they are infringing upon your security. They're using you, deceiving you, and limiting your rights. While this religion still has a value of responsibility (like the upper-right), it is not a responsibility to some objective external moral good but rather a loyalty—or relational responsibility—toward one's in-group.

Donald Trump has been the great high priest of this religion. Consider his most viral campaign slogans: "Build the Wall" invoked a widespread desire for security in the context of borders and immigration. "Drain the Swamp" reflected a deep suspicion of elites and institutions. "Make America Great Again" preached a patriotic nationalism in the face of globalization. Each slogan promised security, seeking to reassert a loyalty to "us first," and resonated deeply with those experiencing or perceiving a loss of jobs, safety, cultural cohesion, or national identity.

Other preachers and prophets include Sean Hannity, nightly stoking the zeal of the faithful on his popular political talk show; celebrities like Roseanne Barr and James Woods, raising the alarm on those who want to take away your rights; and those like Dana White, the head of the UFC (Ultimate Fighting Championship), who claim to be apolitical yet preach that everything you love is under threat but if we band together, we can fight and defeat those trying to destroy our homes and way of life.

Sacred texts for this religion can be found on sites like Fox News, Newsmax, Truth Social, and Breitbart. There have been attempts to build new online fellowship halls for believers to mutually edify one another—such as Parler, Rumble, Gettr, and Gab—but despite strong financial backing, they have been largely unsuccessful in attracting the masses. On the more extreme fundamentalist end, revolutionary zealots are known to congregate underground at places like 8kun, where they can anonymously discuss things like QAnon conspiracy theories, white supremacy, neo-Nazism, racism, anti-Semitism, hate crimes, and other topics (rightly) taboo in respectable society.

The Religion of Security is not restricted to the heartland. A friend of mine who grew up immersed in nineties' hip-hop culture drew my attention to the prominence of such themes. Gangs, for example, prize loyalty to one's group as the highest good. The mentality is, *The streets are dangerous; the police are out to get you; society doesn't understand you. We need to stick together— our safety's at stake.* There is a sacred code of conduct, which is directed not toward a universal moral standard "out there" but rather toward establishing the security of us "in here"—the in-group—through loyalty. There are patriotic signs of identification, such as gang colors and tattoos, that mark one as an insider. The cardinal sin is being a narc, snitch, or traitor—betraying one's crew. It's fascinating how many rappers have expressed respect and admiration for Trump. One wonders whether this ethos is a significant reason why.

Security helps explain why nationalism thrives strongest in this quadrant. While people use the term *nationalism* in different ways, its function in this quadrant is often as an antithesis to (and antidote for) *globalization.* Our integration into the global economy is benefiting our country's wealthy elites, the argument goes, but hurting the working poor. We need to rise up and reassert our voices as the people of this nation and stick up for the common citizen, whose leaders are out of touch and untrustworthy.

For this religion, the temple is the nation. There are heretics within (who need to be shamed or called back to the ancient paths), corrupt leaders above (who need to be overthrown for defiling the sanctuary in D.C.), and hostile invaders at the gate (who need to be repelled with stronger enforcement of our sacred borders).

This helps explain why immigration is such a focal issue for this quadrant. While there is broad consensus that immigration reform is desperately needed, it is a flash-point rally cry for the Religion of Security, for it touches on all the core values mentioned earlier.

Boundaries of purity are also rigidly enforced. Cancel culture is not unique to the lower-left; it's just as strong on the lower-right. Trump excommunicated a long string of comrades on the sheer basis of loyalty, and his protégés do the same. Even before he was elected, Republicans and conservative Christians were being "canceled" if they didn't support him.

This religion has also contributed to what some have called the death of expertise, where the public has lost trust in intellectual authorities. Everyone has a statistic, study, or story to challenge the wisdom of experts. We have more information at our fingertips than ever, so, in the words of Tom Nichols, "average citizens believe themselves to be on an equal intellectual footing with doctors and diplomats."[10] When the postmodern suspicion of authority meets the internet, this revivalist religion sparks a grassroots movement of conspiracy theories, contesting the authority of the misguided priestly class.

So, where do we go?

THE KING'S TABLE

Progress. Responsibility. Identity. Security. There are more than
two parties; there are four—and on their own, they're all pretty
boring.

You're probably asking, *Where does Jesus belong in these four
quadrants?* Well, he doesn't belong to these values. Rather, these
values belong to him.[II] As we'll see in the next chapter, with
Jesus you get the best of progress, responsibility, identity, and
security. He can crash these four parties because they're all
rooted in values that ultimately belong to him. But on their own,
these values are not enough; these gods will not deliver.

Where does the church belong? The church belongs to Jesus.
We are not to be contained by these quadrants. (It's claustrophobic in there!) Rather, the King of kings is throwing a better
party, forming a common table in a conflicted world. His table
has people who lean in all different directions but refuse to bow
to the idols that hold sway.

We need to prioritize Jesus or we're doomed. In the coming
chapters, we'll see *how* to prioritize him, but first let's recognize
the stakes. If we don't, our friendships and families will be fractured, our churches will be divided, and the unity for which
Christ died will be trampled upon. While his church will sur-
vive intact, *your* church—and your faith—may not.

The solution is not to become *a*political. In some ways, I hope
you'll come away from this book *more* political, though in a
healthy way. I'm also not saying the church should be centrist,
always trying to take the middle of the road or path of least resistance. As you'll see, there are definite places to be bold and
take a stand.

Yet there is a powerful opportunity to bear witness to the
prophetic unity of God's kingdom. Pledging our ultimate alle-

giance to Jesus will help us love our neighbors across partisan lines, learn from them, and live peacefully with them. It will bless us with stronger friendships, families, and churches. It will make us a better prophetic witness to Jesus's kingdom party for the world.

Wait a sec. Are you saying I shouldn't listen to NPR? you might be asking. *Or that I can't read Jordan Peterson?* No, I'm not saying to isolate or escape from politics or culture. As a matter of fact, we *need* people who lean in all different directions. We need it because it allows us to help one another see the good and the temptations in our respective areas as we pursue Jesus together.

Jesus shows us how to be actively engaged in politics without destroying our souls. Whichever quadrant we're in, he disrupts politics-as-usual and calls us into a bigger, bolder, grander vision that can redeem our partisan divide.

He crashes the party to bring life to the world.

We've seen how politics is more religious than we think. In the next chapter, we'll explore how the *gospel* is more *political* than many people think—though again not in the way you might expect! Let's move from *describing* the political religions to *prescribing* the kingdom. We want to see what faithfulness to Jesus looks like in the political arena, and how his party is better, as we pledge our ultimate allegiance to the King of kings.

Reflection Questions

- How can you tell when your political views are becoming something closer to a religion?

- Which of the four quadrants do you lean toward and why? If you have a difficult time identifying which one you most relate to, look for the quadrant you think I'm being too hard on. That might be an indicator of which way you lean.

- Which quadrant do you have the hardest time with? What bothers you most about the ideas or people in this quadrant and why?

- Make a list of friends and family members who lean into your least favorite quadrant. What specific steps could you take to better understand them and love them?

- How have your political leanings shifted over time? What were the factors that contributed to your change in perspective?

PLEDGING ALLEGIANCE
TO THE KING OF KINGS

Fifteen years ago, my friend Jim lived in Turkey, where he did some work as a basketball scout. He was helping American players acclimate to the local culture.

Leon, one of those players, was from small-town Kentucky and found himself in the most fundamentalist religious town in Turkey. It was like the Bible Belt of Turkey—or the Quran Belt—with loads of Islamic groups. There weren't many Americans, and Jim knew Leon would have a hard time.

When Jim arrived, Leon opened his door sporting a massive beard and said, "I don't know how to buy razors! They're locked in a case at the store, and I can't speak the language to get them." He was also famished. "I'm hungry! I can't find a restaurant to go to, and I wouldn't even be able to read the menu. I'm so confused. I don't know what to do."

"Don't worry, man," Jim responded. "I'll help you find a restaurant. Is there one that interests you? I'll go with you and help you navigate the menu."

"Yeah," he replied. "I've been visiting this restaurant, but I can't tell when they're open. The people there are nice, but they don't even have tables set up. They talk to me, teach me little

Turkish phrases, and give me some food to eat. But their hours are hit-or-miss."

"Tell me more," Jim said.

"Well, they play this nice spiritual music several times a day."

"Five times a day?"

"Exactly."

"Uh, show me." Jim chuckled, beginning to realize where this was going. Leon pointed out his window to the building.

"Ha!" Jim said. "That's a mosque. Man, you're growing out your beard, showing up there every day, looking for help. Those phrases they were teaching you were the *Shahada*, a phrase you say to convert to Islam."

"Do you mean to tell me," Leon asked, with a shocked look in his eyes, "I became a Muslim and didn't even know it?"

* * *

I don't believe that Leon actually converted to Islam. But it did get me thinking about something much more serious: Can we convert to a religion and not even know? Could we slowly drift away from Jesus as something else becomes our god?

In the previous chapter, I described the four political religions of our day. At first glance, they may look innocuous (like a restaurant), but upon closer inspection, they are religious (like a mosque). These "secular" ideologies are not neutral. The illusion of neutrality prevents us from realizing their danger. They can seduce us into zealous devotion and compete with our allegiance to Jesus.

It's happening all over America. People think they're simply dining in a restaurant but soon find themselves worshipping in a temple. Just as Jim helped Leon understand the culture around him so that he could navigate it more clearly, I want to expose the religious nature of the political reality we take for granted so that we can navigate it more faithfully.

First, however, let's address a common objection: Shouldn't

we just focus on "spiritual" things? Isn't talking about politics a waste of time, distracting us from the more important matters of salvation? Stick to the gospel, many Christians say, and don't get involved in the messy public affairs of the world. A helpful starting point is to recognize that words like *gospel* and *salvation* are political terms, because Jesus is Lord over all.

JESUS IS LORD

"Jesus is Lord"—the central Christian proclamation—is a political statement. It has to do with who is the rightful ruler of the world. In Jesus's day, everyone knew that Caesar was lord. He was the top dog, the man in charge. For example, in the Priene Calendar Inscription, an edict inscribed in stone from 9 B.C., the Roman Empire celebrated this "gospel" (*evangelion*), or good news, of Caesar Augustus's arrival and made his birthday the beginning of the calendar year because

> when everything was falling [into disorder] and tending toward dissolution, [Caesar Augustus] restored it once more and gave to the whole world a new aura. . . . [He was] sent to us and our descendants as Savior, has put an end to war and has set all things in order . . . fulfill[ing] all the hopes of earlier times. . . . We should consider [his arrival] equal to the Beginning of all things.[1]

That's quite a job description! Notice how words like *gospel, Savior,* and *lord*—words we tend to think of as *religious* today—are loaded with *political* significance. They related to ending war and establishing peace, thereby bringing order and justice to the world. Here they were applied to Caesar, but the early church brought a rude awakening: There was a new King in town.

They claimed that Jesus is King *over* Caesar. The New Testament boldly declares that because of his sacrificial death, "God has highly exalted him and bestowed on him the name that is above every name, so that at the name of Jesus every knee should bow . . . and every tongue confess that Jesus Christ is Lord."[2] Upon Jesus's resurrection, God gave him "all authority in heaven and on earth" and established him as "king of kings and lord of lords."[3] Jesus is the desire of the nations, the judge of the living and the dead, and the day is coming when "the kingdoms of this world [will] have become the kingdoms of our Lord and of His Christ, and He shall reign forever and ever!"[4]

We saw in the previous chapter how modern politics is more religious than many people think. Here we see that the gospel is also more political than you might think—though not in the way many people assume.

The church is called not to impose this reign by force but to bear witness to its reality through our shared life and public witness. We're to throw a different kind of party. The church's witness is to follow the way of Jesus, the way of the cross. To do justice, show mercy, and walk humbly with our God.[5] To embody compassion and conviction, with soft hearts and steel spines, speaking the truth in love. To lay down our lives in sacrificial service, faithful witness, and extravagant love—even for our so-called political enemies—because we follow a King who's done the same for us.[6]

That's church politics.

Yet Jesus is not just Lord of your life; he's Lord of the world. God has not just given him your heart; he's given him the nations, exalting him as the rightful ruler of heaven and earth.[7] Presidents and peasants and everyone in between are called to bend the knee before the King of justice and love.

Faith is another politically loaded word. In the ancient world, it meant allegiance.[8] Placing your faith in a leader meant giving them your trust, devotion, and commitment, seeking to align your life with their rule. Putting your *faith* in the *gospel* of Jesus as *Lord* and *Savior* is a political act, responding to a royal message with public implications.

Certainly, Christ calls us to a different way of life than the worldly leaders who "lord it over" one another.[9] (More on that in the chapters to come.) Christ exercises his kingdom authority in a different manner than the politics we're used to. Yet it is foolish to pretend that Christ's kingdom is simply a private matter for personal devotion rather than one that lays claim to the public life of the world.

One reason some people miss these political associations with the gospel today is the sacred/secular divide. We tend to divvy life up into *secular* things (like politics and culture and work) and *sacred* things (like religion and spirituality). The former are about the public life of the world, with facts we all share. The latter are about private affairs and beliefs, with values for personal devotion. We imagine a rigid barrier between these two categories, and never the twain shall meet. We put Jesus in the "sacred" box, effectively banishing him from the bulk of "secular" life.

Yet the gospel isn't having it. For Jewish ears, *lord* meant "God." *Yahweh*, the Hebrew name for God, was translated into Greek as "Lord." So, "Jesus is Lord" means he is God in the flesh, Yahweh come to save his people.[10] Jesus is the incarnation of the Lord described in the Old Testament as "the great King over all the earth," who "reigns over the nations" and "is seated on his holy throne."[11] Jesus's exaltation to the right hand of God's heavenly throne means he's now in charge. There's no higher party, no greater political authority than that.

Jesus is not only Lord *over* Caesar, but he's the LORD who *is* God. Jesus rules.

THE TRUE KING

Placing your faith in Jesus means pledging allegiance to the King of kings. When you reject Christ as Lord, you begin looking to various Caesars to take his place. (Or you might use "Jesus language" to justify the Caesar you *really* serve.) This is the root of the four political religions: Each takes something good God has given and exalts it above God. It displaces the Giver with one of his gifts. Progress. Responsibility. Identity. Security. These are all things God has given us in creation. They make good gifts but terrible masters. Let's see how.

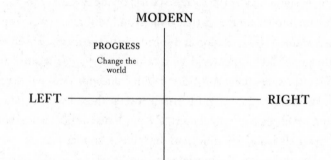

There are good things in the *Progress* quadrant. Progress is a true gift of God. The biblical story starts in a garden and ends in a city—creation is *going* somewhere. In Genesis, God calls humanity to work and keep the garden, cultivating the hidden potential of God's world.[12] That has often been called the cultural mandate; God commissions us to *cultivate culture.* As the nineteenth-century Reformed theologian Abraham Kuyper poetically puts it,

> God crowns [creation] with humanity. They awaken its life, arouse its powers, and with human hands bring to light the glory that lay locked in its depths.[13]

Without progress, we wouldn't have electricity, modern medicine, or air-conditioning (the latter particularly crucial when we lived in Arizona). Our lives would likely be shorter and more painful. Modern science, technology, and institutions have radically raised the standard of living around the world. We have more food, better education, and greater prosperity than any previous generation. I'm a fan of civilization.

But this apple has a bite in it—and it's not always clear whether the fruit is from the tree of life or of the knowledge of good and evil. When progress becomes an idol—displacing God as an ultimate commitment—it requires human sacrifice and can end up depleting life. Consider Facebook, which intends to bring the world together but ends up tearing us apart. Or food engineering, intended to feed the world but now being used to make unhealthy food more addictive. Nuclear energy has the potential to power the world but can also destroy it.

Humans are made to seek progress, but when we make it an idol, we sacrifice one another on its altar. We must retain the benefits of progress but not allow it to become an independent ideology that cuts us off from God as the deeper source of life. Have you allowed progress to become an idol detached from your commitment to Jesus as Lord?

Then there's the *Responsibility* quadrant. Is there great value here? Absolutely. Responsibility is a good thing. God blessed

Adam and Eve with a garden to steward, a family to raise, and a personal stake in the task of tending the world. God gives us moral agency, with a prospect of reward or punishment. Wisdom is a major theme in Scripture—the way of virtue that leads to flourishing when the world is working as it should.

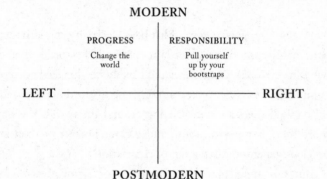

Wickedness—irresponsible behavior—threatens to burn society down. Our depravity reinforces the need for strong checks and balances against individual vice, business corruption, and governmental tyranny. The upper-right quadrant contains many valuable insights on the nature of the world.

Yet when we give idol status to responsibility, there can be a temptation to ignore the biblical call to justice. This leads to human sacrifice, evident in how some of us can think about people who are struggling. We may have a tendency to look down on single parents who are trying to make ends meet, homeless people who are struggling with mental illness, or people medicating pain through substance abuse. This aloofness can be justified with mantras like "You get what you deserve," "If they just had better parents," and "If they only worked a little harder, they'd be fine."

Responsibility is good, but when it displaces God as the organizing principle for an entire worldview, it overshadows grace and drowns out compassion. It becomes a god who says, *It's all about how hard you work and being responsible for yourself and your family.* It can reduce the world's problems down to moral corruption, a lack of responsibility, and the failure of the family.

We are made for responsibility but also for more. It's important that we retain the benefits of responsibility while not allowing it to become an idol that displaces the God of grace. Have you allowed responsibility to become an idol that competes with your allegiance to Jesus as Lord?

Next, there's the *Identity* quadrant. As with the previous two quadrants, there is good here. Identity is integral to the gospel. We are created in the image of God, with inestimable dignity, value, and worth. We are made to know ourselves as the beloved of God, who goes all the way to hell and back to be with us forever. On the first page of the Bible, male and female are already speaking to the nuances of identity. In the pages that follow, God cares for and honors our different ethnic backgrounds in the rise of the nations, so much so that in the end, his kingdom is one where every nation, tribe, and tongue flourishes, where their identity isn't stripped from them but is blessed in the multicultural diversity of the people of God.[14]

MODERN

| PROGRESS | RESPONSIBILITY |
| Change the world | Pull yourself up by your bootstraps |

LEFT ———————————————— RIGHT

| IDENTITY | |
| Live your truth | |

POSTMODERN

Identity is a good thing, but when it becomes ultimate, it becomes destructive. In attempting to deconstruct broken systems, this religion can go too far. It can dismantle things God intentionally designed into his creation that are integral to our flourishing. The husband who sees the institution of marriage as a barrier to his happiness commits adultery and tears the fabric of his family apart, saying, "Wouldn't God want me to be happy?" The disillusioned twentysomething who sees no good in their country sets an immigrant's small business aflame to vent their anger in a riot, ironically, over injustice toward the vulnerable. Or when my close friend's mom was pregnant with him, as a poor teenager, and everyone told her, "You just need to end this pregnancy, so you can live your dreams and be happy." Thankfully, she didn't listen.

This religion is, arguably, contributing to escalating rates of anxiety and depression.[15] We were made to *receive* our identity from outside ourselves, not primarily *create* it from within. To act *from* our identity as beloved rather than work *for* our identity as beloved. When identity comes solely from within, our world threatens to fall apart. Social cohesion is lost as we sacrifice one another on the altar of our self-creation projects. When you peek beneath the veneer of humility in this religion ("You do you; who am I to tell you what to do?"), it cultivates a pride and arrogance before others and, ultimately, before God ("I am the Great I Am; who are you to tell me who to be?").

How do we retain the power of identity yet not allow it to become an idol that distorts our perspective of ourselves, the world, and God? Have you allowed identity to become an idol that defines you more than Jesus does?

Finally, we come to the *Security* quadrant. There are definitely good things here, too. Security is good. Adam and Eve dwelled together in safety, with a garden to protect. God gives rules and boundaries for our good, which allow us to work, raise families, and build community without threat. God is a defender who is out to establish the security of his people and protect his kingdom from evil.[16] Security is a good thing.

But when it becomes ultimate, it creates a religion whose idols require sacrifice. So often, what is seen as a shield to protect oneself and one's family is shaped into a sword that preemptively attacks others. This ideology can lead to ethnic, political, and religious violence.

What does this look like? It's the death threats one of our pastors received when we as a church started helping refugees long ago. It's the graffiti on the side of a mosque or a synagogue that says, "Go back to where you came from." It's Dylann Roof walking into a predominantly black church and interrupting a prayer meeting with gunshots. Such horrors are fundamentalist extremism, an ideology that requires the human sacrifice of people made in God's image.

We want to retain the benefits of security without allowing it to become an independent ideology that hardens us toward those who are different or outside our in-group. Have you allowed security to become an idol that competes for your ultimate security in Jesus as Lord?

Let's make explicit something that's been implicit so far: Each of the political religions is rooted in idolatry.

IDEOLOGY AS IDOLATRY

Having idols is an attempt to replace God. Here's how it works. First, idolatry takes a good thing God has made and moves it into an ultimate place to which we give our devotion and allegiance. Ancient idols were associated with some good aspects of creation: wealth and prosperity, sexual pleasure and fertility, power and strength. In their proper place, those are all gifts of God for the flourishing of our world. When we elevate these good things over God, however, they function as idols—even without the carved stone statues.

Similarly, each political quadrant has a key value at its center. Progress. Responsibility. Identity. Security. Those are all, as we've seen, good gifts of God rooted in his creational design. Yet each can be elevated over him. When this happens, the gift morphs into an idol that becomes an organizing principle for the world, effectively functioning as idolatry. This gives rise to a political religion.[17]

That's how I'm using these terms in this book: The *idol* is the thing or value we substitute in the place of God as the organizing principle for the world; the *ideology* is the view of the world that forms around that substitute to justify its centrality and organize the world around it; the *religion* is the rituals and rhythms, the formational practices observed by those who center their lives around this idol, effectively competing with their allegiance to Jesus.

Idols come with religious rituals. While we might see these

rituals as meaningless practices, they shape their practitioners over time. The habits form our hearts and change our character. Scripture says that those who make idols become like them.[18] At first, we make these little statues, but then they end up making us. Those who worship war become violent, those who worship money become greedy, and so on. The practices shape us.

We become what we worship.

Similarly, each political religion has its religious rituals. In the previous chapter, we looked at each quadrant's priests and prophets, its sacred texts and symbolic temples. Each partisan camp has its own national liturgies and tests of devotion, its forms of catechesis to instruct the faithful, proselytization to evangelize the masses, and excommunication to kick out those who transgress the purity boundaries. Each shapes and forms the worshipper into the image of the idol at its center.

Idols always require sacrifice. If you wanted the ancient gods to bless you, you first had to give them gifts. You had to demonstrate your allegiance, curry favor, and keep in good standing. Sometimes the gifts were simple, other times more serious—like human sacrifice. The ancient god Molek essentially said, "I'll give you good crops, but you gotta give me some babies." Idols come at a human cost, unleashing suffering and destruction downstream while unraveling our world as we distance ourselves from God.

Similarly, the political religions demand increasing zeal and devotion, elevating a particular aspect of human flourishing but suppressing others, in a way that ends up sacrificing some people's well-beings on the altar of their devotion. The religions promise salvation but unleash destruction. We must recognize that the partisan idols are out to divide the body of the church and the common good of society, fracturing both into a battle of Us versus Them.

And it's working.

POLITICS IS THE NEW RELIGION

Politics has become the new religion. We have become like the people of Samuel's day, who demanded, "Give us a king, that we may be like the other nations."[19] They wanted the power, prestige, and peace of mind offered by the world's ruthless political powers. Yet God responded, "They have rejected me as their king."[20] Placing such great trust in the mighty Caesars of our day is—whether we recognize it or not—a rejection of God as King. This is true even if we use God language to justify the real Caesar we serve.

This helps explain why it seems everyone has gone so crazy: We've lost the horizon of the kingdom. As political theologian Oliver O'Donovan has demonstrated, when you have God "above" you (as a higher authority over the public life of our world) and his kingdom "before" you (with the assurance of future hope that things will ultimately be put right in the end), it puts things in proper perspective.[21]

You can be involved in politics, but it's not everything. If your side loses, God is still sovereign and in control. The world may be a mess, but God's future is coming. If your side wins, you can be humble and gracious—there's a bigger picture at stake.

When you reject God as King, however, politics can turn out to be your only hope. Without the grand horizon of his kingdom, the world becomes more compressed, shrunk, restricted. All your eggs are now in that basket. Everything's riding on the next election, on getting this policy enacted or that person in office. So we take off the gloves and fight for victory, no holds barred.

Politics *is* important—but not *that* important. It can't bear the weight of transcendence, pressure of meaning, and assurance of hope that a world without God places upon it. Only God's kingdom can handle that. It's like placing a naval aircraft carrier on the back of a donkey or elephant: Either will buckle under the load.

A recent article from *The Atlantic,* called "Breaking Faith," argues that our national decline in church attendance has affected our political posture.[22] The author is not a Christian, as far as I know, yet he observed how on the Right, it is those who don't regularly attend church who are most likely to believe that character doesn't matter in leaders or who are more hostile to African Americans, Latinos, and Muslims. They might identify as Christian (or even "evangelical," that increasingly ambiguous polling label), but they're disconnected from the church. To paraphrase political commentator Ross Douthat, if you didn't like the religious right, wait until you meet the irreligious right.[23]

The Left is not excluded from the same critique. The article contrasts the strong religious roots of the historic civil rights movement with today's activism. We see hatred and violence espoused, with calls for "blood on the streets" and revolution rather than reform. Could it be that as our society has increasingly rejected God, we've become more vicious and hostile in our culture wars?

This makes sense. When we reject God as King, it can leave a vacuum of competition for political power. Friedrich Nietzsche, the famous nineteenth-century atheist philosopher who laid the foundations for postmodernism, predicted this. "I am dynamite," he said, foreseeing what the rejection of God would do to society, as politics "becomes entirely absorbed into the realm of spiritual warfare. . . . There will be wars the like of which have never been seen on earth before. Only after me will there be grand politics on earth."[24] He foresaw the great world wars and spiritual fervor of our battles for control over society. That's not a party I want to belong to. Get rid of God and that's all that's left.

Grand politics.

A bleak world indeed. It's worth noting that spiritual warfare is still part of this picture. "Our struggle is not against flesh and blood," the apostle Paul reminds us, "but against the rulers, against the authorities, against the powers of this dark world and against the spiritual forces of evil in the heavenly realms."[25] Our battle is not against people ("flesh and blood"), but we are to be alert to the dark spiritual forces at work behind the division and devastation around us. The spiritual and political realms are not isolated but intertwined, wreaking havoc in our world's distance from the kingdom of God.[26]

Have you rejected God as your King? Are you using God language but really serving another Caesar? Is your ultimate trust in the way of the elephant or the way of the donkey (which can both easily succumb to the way of the dragon), or is your trust in the way of the Lamb? Our devotion is not to King Biden or King Trump but King Jesus. If you are in Christ, your ultimate allegiance is not to the Democratic Party or the Republican Party but to the kingdom of God. This King throws a better party.

This doesn't mean Christians won't have political opinions, but it might mean we won't fit comfortably within partisan lines. We'll look in the coming chapters at how to know when to plant flags on particular political positions and how to carry those convictions with Christlike character. We'll explore creative ways to be political that don't fit the common boxes or national narratives. Yet whichever quadrant you lean toward, following Jesus is going to be countercultural today.

This is a clarion call to action: to put Jesus back at the center of the church's politics—of *your* politics—even if that means crashing some party lines. To pledge your allegiance to the world's true King.

Jesus is the King of kings and the only One worthy of that

place. He's our endgame. Our goal is to reform church politics—that is, how the church *does* politics—by putting Jesus back at the center. Not to be *a*political but to be *rightly* political. We dethrone the idols to exalt the King of kings. Jesus is Lord, the rightful ruler over all creation, exalted over heaven and earth. Each of us is called to bend the knee before the King of justice and love.

The King who invites you to his table.

COME TO THE TABLE

We're all hungry for a better world. That's what drives us to the political religions: hunger. We're like Leon, who left his house in Turkey because he was famished and looking for a meal but ended up almost accidentally converting to another religion in a mosque. While that's a playful story, many of us have left the home we were made for with God because we had a hunger—a deep longing—we sought to fill. We entered the sanctuary of the political religions because we thought they could satiate us.[27]

Yet the political religions will ultimately leave us empty. The problem isn't our hunger; it's where we're going to satisfy it. Jesus invites us to bring our hunger to him. He's the only One who can really fill it, can meet our deepest longings in a way that the idols and ideologies can't. He sets a common table in a conflicted world and calls us to come and feast with him. At the Lord's Supper, the King of the universe feeds us with himself, the bread of his body given and wine of his blood shed, offering communion as the Lamb, who was slain for our redemption. So bring your hunger for a better world, and come to the table of the King.

To those who are tempted by the idol of Progress, I know you hunger for a day when sickness, disease, suffering, and poverty are no more. When all things will be made right. You long for that one technique or innovation that will change everything. But there will never be a pill or invention that can fully meet that longing. What we ultimately need is more than a pill; it's a person, and that person is Jesus. He is the One who will wipe away every tear from every eye as he makes all things new. He will put disease in remission, turn weapons of war into instruments of peace, and make the finest feast for those who are hungry. Come to Jesus; feast at his table.[28]

To those tempted by the idol of Responsibility, I know you hunger for a peaceful life, where if you just work hard enough and live a morally upright life, you can have the American dream of prosperity and peace. But there's that sneaking suspicion something could go wrong. So you put in the extra hours, find the right schools, save your money, and eat your salads. You work hard and take responsibility, but it's not enough. You cannot outrun sin, suffering, and death. Yet there is good news: It's not about your responsibility and work; it's about Jesus and how he took responsibility for you in his life, death, and resurrection and how he is inviting you to an eternal family and feast based upon his work. Come and feast with him.

To those tempted by the idol of Identity, I know you are hungry to be seen, known, and loved. It can be hard to figure out who you are in this world. But Christ invites you to rest. Rest from the toil of self-creation; of trying to have the right causes, perfect career, and presentable image; of trying to construct a self that's worthy of being seen. Because the One who created you knows you intimately in all the nuances of your story, he sees you deeply and loves you immensely. He's the very same King who is pursuing you and fights for you on his mission to bring justice to every place of oppression and restoration to all who are trampled or overlooked. Come feast at his table.

To those tempted by Security, I know you are hungry for a life where the things you most care about are not under threat. And you are right: There are outsiders who threaten the things you love. But don't blame the wrong outsiders. The true outsiders are sin, Satan, and death.[29] They are hostile invaders in God's good creation. And you are right: Somebody needs to step up and deal with them. The good news is that Someone already has; armed with his perfect life, his victorious death, and his glorified, risen body, Jesus fought the fight you could not win. He was loyal to you when you were not loyal to him. He welcomed you to his table when you were an outsider, inviting you to find a peace that is eternally secure and can never be taken away. Come to his table and feast.

Jesus invites you to join the party. To come to his table, where he gives you himself. The King of kings welcomes you to feast on his presence, to be united with him and his people, to taste the beginning of the world made new in the intimacy and power of communion with him. So bend the knee before the world's true King, pledge your allegiance to his kingdom, and then come to his table and feast.

Come to Jesus.

Reflection Questions

- Are there times when your political engagement has felt like religious devotion competing with your allegiance to Jesus? Pray and ask God to search your heart to reveal such moments. (The goal here is not shame but honesty before God with our stories.)

- Why is it important to acknowledge the good intentions of those we disagree with politically?

- Since each quadrant reflects some aspect of God's creational design, each will contain good gifts that should be affirmed. Identify some good aspects of each quadrant and thank God for those gifts. Try to go beyond the examples I mentioned in the chapter.

- Since each quadrant has been influenced by the Fall, each will contain some very destructive features. Identify some sinful and broken aspects of each quadrant and pray for God to rescue people from the tyranny of idolatry.

- How does Jesus provide what each political religion promises but can't fulfill?

WELCOME TO THE KING'S TABLE

"Why are there All Lives Matter posters all over your church?"

"What All Lives Matter posters?" we responded.

"You guys have All Lives Matter posters plastered all over your property."

We were confused. Had someone graffitied our building? Had local activists plastered signs on our campus? "Show us these posters," we said. He led us outside and pointed to a massive sign—one of many on our property—that boasted our church's vision statement, a vision we've held for more than a decade.

All of Life is All for Jesus.

Ha! How did he get *that* from *this*? we wondered. Those big bold letters were being radically misread. It became clear as we talked further: He was a convert to the Religion of Identity (postmodern-left). He had recently left his church (a good church we knew of) because they did not align strongly enough with the tenets of his newfound faith. He had heard positive things about our church—that we cared for justice and the poor (which is true)—so he'd recently begun visiting. He was greatly distressed, however, as he gazed upon our sign, that we would be for "that" side. His political religion was clouding his vision.

There was a massive gap between what we were saying and what he was hearing.

I've seen a lot of this in recent years. It's not just a problem on the Left (not by a long shot); the Right does the same thing. A pastor friend was recently approached by an irate woman after he mentioned "progressive sanctification" in a sermon. (This is the historic Christian belief that our sanctification, or growth in holiness, doesn't occur overnight but rather is a progressive, or gradual, process.) She blasted, "Why are you saying if I'm being sanctified it means I'll become more progressive?"

Upon listening further, it became clear she had converted to the Religion of Security (postmodern-right). Her zeal for her newfound faith prevented her from listening charitably and caused her to read things that were not being said into what she heard. She was not alone; two angry emails that week shared her same misunderstanding of the sermon.

These stories might be humorous, but the situation they illustrate is not: Political religions are driving the new church split.

* * *

Churches are fracturing along political fault lines. One of the easiest ways to grow a church these days is to plant a flag in one of the political quadrants.[1] Many churches talk only or primarily about the issues important to one quadrant, using the same rhetoric of vitriol and disdain for the "other" side while ignoring or minimizing the faults and shortcomings of their own camp. They grow exponentially as converts to the new political religions flock to their church.

It's working. I've seen this in the Phoenix area, a politically diverse region. Leaders have launched sermon series like marketing campaigns, preaching to their particular quadrant and attacking other churches who are not as "bold" as they are. Congregants have sorted themselves into churches that plant a flag in their particular camp. We're in danger of having four new denominations: what we could call a Progress Church, a Responsibility Church, an Identity Church, and a Security Church.[2] They're growing like crazy, and I, for one, see these as worse parties, not better ones.

All this because we're no longer able to stay at the table together—the King's table. This raises an important question: How do we stay together in a culture that's tearing us apart?

LEANING VERSUS BOWING

Jesus invites you to bring your *lean* but submit your *bow*. "Leaning" is where you have a different perspective; "bowing" is where you have a different allegiance. We all have political leanings— that's great. We need one another and, with those leanings, are stronger together in the body of Christ. The danger is when that lean becomes a bow, a different center of your life that competes with your allegiance to Jesus and becomes a functional religion.[3]

Jesus calls disciples with different political leanings. In the Gospels, he gathered followers who were (revolutionary) Zealots, (status quo) tax collectors, (blue-collar) fishermen, and (white-collar) doctors. Sure, our modern political categories don't map exactly onto the ancient world, yet there is significant overlap. Let's use four of Jesus's disciples as rough icons for each of the four quadrants as we explore some of their underlying values and ideals.

Zealots and Tax Collectors

First, Simon was a Zealot,[4] part of a revolutionary party who stood against the establishment of Rome. I like to think of him as an icon for the Identity quadrant. The Zealots confronted injustice, calling out the empire's exploitation of vulnerable people. They also stood against ideological impurity, confronting the polytheism that corrupted the integrity of the faithful. So, they were a bit like Bernie Bros (shouting down the system) and left-wing campus professors (policing ideological purity). They also despised compromisers, those Jews who worked together with the Roman establishment.

The Zealots were politically aggressive. In A.D. 6 (not long after Jesus's birth), they organized a mass protest against the Roman census in Galilee (where Jesus was from). They saw Jewish participation in the census as an implicit acknowledgment of the empire's right to rule their homeland. Later, shortly after Jesus's death, the Zealots led the first revolt against Rome at Masada (A.D. 66–70), where many of them committed mass suicide rather than surrender the fortress they occupied (A.D. 73). They were hardcore.

Zealot extremists were known as Sicarii ("dagger men") because they used daggers to publicly assassinate Jewish leaders who collaborated with Rome. (And you thought Antifa was bad!)

So, Simon was a revolutionary when Jesus called him.

Matthew, meanwhile, was a tax collector who worked *for* the Roman establishment.[5] The Responsibility quadrant's not a perfect fit, but stay with me for a minute. Tax collectors were free agents in the international market. They took money from fellow Jews, like IRS agents. Only rather than pay them a salary, Rome simply expected tax collectors to take a cut for themselves, and they gladly obliged. So, the attitude was, *It's not my job to change the system. I just need to be responsible for myself and take care of those close to me. If everyone else did that, we'd be fine.*

Tax collectors were wealthy, corrupt, and hated by the revolution-minded Zealots. We see this in the Gospels, where tax collectors are regularly equated with sinners, prostitutes, and pagans (groups despised in that culture).[6] Rabbinic tradition equated them with robbers. When Zacchaeus, "a chief tax collector [who] was wealthy," began to follow Jesus, he gave back to all he had defrauded.[7] Tax collectors likely needed security and therefore lived in the ancient equivalent of gated communities. Neighbors saw them as traitors who cared only about their self-advancement rather than the good of their people.

So, that's where Matthew was coming from when Jesus called him to the table.

Here's the point: Zealots and tax collectors hated each other! Matthew worked for the very system Simon stood against. Don't miss the impact of Jesus calling a Zealot and a tax collector to follow him—together! That would be like inviting a militant activist and a military general into his crew. Or an Occupy Wall Streeter and a Wall Street CEO into his small group. Imagine inviting Alexandria Ocasio-Cortez and Ben Shapiro over to your dinner party and expecting them to become best friends because they share you in common.

The King invites both to his party.

Imagine those campfire conversations! I love to think of the disciples, after a long day of ministry, processing everything together. The recent TV series *The Chosen* does a good job depicting some of the tension we'd expect between the disciples, given their various perspectives. It's not like their political leanings went away once they began following Jesus.

Jesus confronted the "bow" of both. To the Zealot, his challenge was to love your enemies, pray for those who persecute you, forsake violent revolution, and spend more time removing

the plank from your own eye than the speck from your brother's.[8] To the tax collector, Jesus's challenge was to forsake your
love of money—which is the root of all evil and chief rival to
God—and live generously, not hoarding up wealth on earth,
where moth and rust destroy, but rather making friends with the
poor and storing up treasure in heaven.[9]

Like Simon and Matthew, you're called to give up your "bow"
in order to give your fullest allegiance to Jesus. Yet it doesn't stop
there.

Jesus also fulfilled the "lean" of each. To the Zealot, he offered
a countercultural revolution in an alternative community that
embodied the justice of God, that peaceably invaded the old
order of things and worked its way, like yeast, into the dough of
a corrupt society to permeate it from the inside out. To the tax
collector, he offered a truer, eternal security in a kingdom that
cannot be shaken, where those who give all receive much more
in return—family, friends, fields, and finances—in this life as
well as the age to come.[10]

Jesus confronts your bow but fulfills your lean. What you're
looking for in the political quadrants is more meaningfully fulfilled in Jesus. You've got to leave your idols at the door, but
there's a better party inside. Okay, we've still got two more quadrants to go.

Doctors and Fishermen

Jesus also calls blue-collar fishermen and white-collar doctors.
Peter was a fisherman,[11] used to strenuous work with long hours.
Fishermen typically worked the night shift, casting their nets in
the dark so fish wouldn't see (and avoid) their nets. They needed
strength and endurance to haul in the nets and sort through
their catch in the morning, and they were business savvy as they

sold in the local market to keep their small boat and crew afloat amid competition.

I like to think of Peter as an icon for the Security quadrant. He's the gruff, rugged small-business owner—a straight shooter who says what he thinks, doesn't back down from a fight, and values a hard day's work. He's loyal, the one who'll pull out a sword and face down a battalion to defend the ones he loves. Although he cares about his nation, it's the smaller circles of his more immediate community, with thicker bonds of proximate relationship, where his deepest loyalty lies.

Luke, meanwhile, was "the beloved physician,"[12] a highly educated doctor.[13] While not one of the original twelve disciples, Luke was an influential early follower of Jesus who wrote more than a quarter of the New Testament, more than any other author.[14] He probably came from money, to afford the professional training of his day. It's likely he wanted to use that position to serve the world, both as a doctor and in service to the fledgling Jesus movement.

I like to think of Luke as an icon for the Progress quadrant. He's the deep-thinking intellectual, the refined scholar, who is good with words and loves books. He wants to use his privilege to help humanity and bring healing. He can often be found staring into space, reflecting on all that the disciples have learned from Jesus and how to pass it on for posterity, stewarding a movement that's emerging into an institution with the power to change the world.

Although Jesus challenged both Peter and Luke, he also fulfilled—at a deeper level—their callings. Jesus is the Fisher of Men, who turned Peter into an evangelist who would lead the early church. Jesus is the Great Physician, who invited Luke into an even greater healing he'd come to bring the world. (Luke may not have met Christ in person, but the risen and ascended

Christ called him by his Spirit and he calls us as his followers too.) Like he did with Simon and Matthew, Jesus both confronted their bow and fulfilled their lean.

The point is this: Jesus's disciples were politically diverse.

And Jesus *intentionally* called this motley crew together. He didn't accidentally let a Zealot slip past his radar; his calling of Matthew wasn't a mistake; Peter's brashness didn't catch him by surprise; Luke's passions weren't incidental to his calling. Jesus intentionally invited each of these to follow him—not only because they needed him, but because they needed each other. Like my friend Kyle from high school, Jesus was forming a diverse community from a variety of backgrounds. Jesus was throwing a better party. And it doesn't stop with Zealots, tax collectors, fishermen, and doctors.

It continues with us.

A (POLITICALLY) DIVERSE COMMUNITY

We have different leanings. We come from different backgrounds and experiences. We bring different perspectives to the table. That's a good thing. Jesus invites our lean.

The King gathers us *intentionally*. He's creating a reconciled community, calling all types of people to himself. The apostle Paul famously declared, "In Christ, there is neither Jew nor Gentile, neither slave nor free, nor is there male and female." And, we could add, neither Zealot nor tax collector. Jesus breaks down barriers of ethnicity ("Jew nor Gentile"), class ("slave nor free"), sex ("male and female"), and political party (Democrat and Republican).

Why? The apostle continued, "For you are all one in Christ Jesus."[15]

Jesus died to reconcile a (politically) diverse people. We're stronger together.

On our leadership team, I grew up in the Progress quadrant, Jim in the Responsibility quadrant. Cara leans Identity quadrant; Evan leans Security quadrant. We can get into it with each other! We have spirited disagreements. But we don't seek to ignore or pretend our leanings aren't there; rather, we bring our distinct perspectives to Jesus's common table as a community of his disciples.

We bring our lean, but we're seeking to submit our bow to Jesus. We need each other. I need Jim to point out my idols. Cara and Evan see my blind spots more clearly than I do. Sometimes I see theirs. We're like iron mutually sharpening iron. As we've sought to navigate the political craziness of the past few years, it's been invaluable to lean into one another rather than away. We love one another and, even in the middle of disagreement, seek to lean into the strength of our relationships. When we have a level of trust with people and talk politics with them, we should expect that they have something to teach us. We should strive to listen and assume the best about them and their motives. We should assume positive intent. Be wary of the echo chamber; it's dangerous there.

We're stronger together.

The church needs your leaning. We need people who lean toward *progress* to help us keep cultivating the world, toward *responsibility* to help us care for work and family, toward *identity* to help us be attentive to God's call for justice, and toward *security* to help keep us bold and courageous. If you're a Christian, the goal is not to become disinterested in politics or as centrist as possible. Far from it.

Bring your lean; we need it.

But submit your bow. We are in danger of having a Responsibility Church for Matthew and the moneymakers in Free America, a Progress Church for Luke and the professionals in Smart America, an Identity Church for Simon and the modern-day Zealots in Just America, and a Security Church for Peter and the tough guys in Real America.

These are the four new denominations. They reveal that, more than theological differences, it is political and cultural differences that are fracturing the contemporary church. We are facing a crisis of political discipleship, in which we need Christians equipped to stay together (with unity, not uniformity) amid diverse political leanings. Resist the partisan pull. Stay at the table.

Healthy political discipleship means your relationships will cross party lines. You'll have strong convictions, but you won't fit into the world's boxes. Your positions won't completely conform to the Democratic Party or the Republican Party but increasingly to the kingdom of God. You won't be ultimately beholden to the donkey or the elephant but to the Lamb.

Jesus didn't die so you could hang out with your like-minded buddies; he died to gather all types of people to himself and to one another. Don't trample on the unity for which Christ died. He didn't give his life to make the church an echo chamber; he did it to inaugurate a reconciling kingdom. To establish a community of male and female, slave and free, rich and poor, weak and strong, every nation, tribe, and tongue—and yes, Democrats and Republicans.

So, how can you tell when your lean is becoming a bow?

STAY AT THE TABLE

It's not always easy to tell the difference between leaning and bowing. In the next few chapters, we'll get practical with some

Christian *positions* we should consider for a faithful political witness and the Christlike *character* we need to hold those positions well. But right now let's consider a few questions to help assess whether your lean has become a bow.[16]

First, do you give more time and attention to political pundits than to the words of Scripture? Do they carry more weight with you? Are you editing your Bible based on your party's platform, elevating some parts and downplaying others? That's a good sign of a bow.

Second, as we walked through the quadrants in the previous few chapters, which did you feel the need to defend or justify? Perhaps you thought, *No, that one is not that bad.* If you felt anger, that could be a good indicator you've got an idol. Maybe it's similar to the anger in Acts 19 when Paul challenged the idols of the Ephesians and a riot broke out in the city. Pay attention to that.

Third, do you have a pattern of cutting people out of your life who disagree with your politics? Are there family members you no longer speak to because of something they posted on Facebook? Friends you avoid because they must be stupid or evil to hold "that" position? A church you left because you took offense at a comment someone made?

One of the strongest signs your lean has become a bow is your quickness to break fellowship over such divisions, to look with hatred and animosity toward your brothers and sisters in the body of Christ. Beware this strong sign of a bow.

Fourth, is there a cultural leader who moves your heart more than Jesus? You might say, *No, I've never experienced that,* yet you spend more time listening to Joe Rogan or MrBeast, Bernie Sanders or Steven Crowder, than to just about anyone else. It's easy to look back at a day when you were filled with warmth and affection for Jesus, but now that's waned (I've been there before) as he's been replaced by another whose voice has become more prominent and influential in your life. That's a telltale sign of a bow.

Here's the thing: The false religions don't satisfy. Like all idols, they'll give a short-term high but the rush runs out in the long run. They land in a crash and then burn. Perhaps you're filled with anxiety about the hopeless state of the world, looking down on people you used to love and care for, filled with fear and growing more and more locked in with a political figure or movement to rescue and save you—converting to a religion and not even knowing it.

Yet Jesus creates a common table in a conflicted world. He invites you to bring your anxiety and fears, your leanings and longings, to find their deepest fulfillment in him. He crashes our lame parties in order to build us up and call us into a better one. He calls you to submit your bow to him, giving your deepest allegiance to his kingdom, for the public life of the world. The King welcomes you—with a wide and wild array of others—to his reconciling table.

Reflection Questions

- When have you experienced strained relationships due to political differences? How have you navigated these conflicts? Is there a step you can take to help repair a broken relationship?

- There's a difference between having a political leaning and bowing to an idol. Prayerfully reflect on each of the following questions and ask God to reveal any evidence of idolatry.

  - Do you give more time and attention to political pundits than to the words of Scripture?
  - Is there a quadrant you feel the need to defend or justify and are unwilling to let be challenged?
  - Do you have a pattern of refusing to talk to people who disagree with your politics? Have you ever cut someone out of your life because of politics?
  - How do we know when we are giving too much attention to a political leader?

- Ask God to show you if there are patterns you need to confess and repent of, and any steps you can take to repair broken relationships.

TEN POLITICAL COMMANDMENTS

"Will you sign the King of Kings Commitment?" Going into the last election season, our leadership team asked our church to join us in signing this ten-point commitment we created in order to highlight how our allegiance to Jesus—the King of kings—should shape our political engagement. This was not about what opinions to hold but rather how to hold them well.

People signed on in droves. The commitment helped create clarity around God's expectations for our *character* in political engagement. It shaped our political discussions in ways that preserved relationships that otherwise would have been fraught or maybe even destroyed. It kept the political religions from crashing our kingdom party.

We jokingly referred to these as the Ten Political Commandments. Tongue in cheek because we didn't want them to be confused with the *actual* Ten Commandments. Yet we *do* believe that God commands these things in Scripture. They are not optional add-ons for God's people but direct orders from Christ our King. So they carry gravity.

Sadly, many today believe Christlike character doesn't apply in the political arena. *Yeah, God commands such character for our personal lives, but it's unrealistic out here in the real world.* That's a lie from the pit of hell. *All* of life is all for Jesus, including the political arena.

In this chapter, I want to explore a Jesus-shaped political character and the powerful potential such character has to counterculturally witness to Christ's greater kingdom. I'll list the ten political commandments from our King of Kings Commitment here, then spend the rest of the chapter exploring each one.

THE KING OF KINGS COMMITMENT

1. **Worship:** I commit my allegiance to King Jesus over all idols and ideologies. (Exodus 20:2–3; Psalm 115:1–8; Philippians 2:9–11)

2. **Love of Neighbor:** I commit to participating in civic life as a means of loving and serving my neighbor rather than just serving my own interests. (Matthew 22:34–40; Philippians 2:1–11)

3. **Image of God:** I commit to honoring the image of God in all people by treating them with respect and abstaining from dehumanizing caricatures. (Genesis 1:26; James 3:9)

4. **Biblical Wisdom:** I commit to having my views challenged by the biblical story rather than using the Bible to proof-text my predetermined positions. (Psalm 119; 2 Timothy 3:16)

5. **Biblical Justice:** I commit to understanding and pursuing justice as I engage in civic life, not minimizing Scripture's repeated call to seek justice, and allowing Scripture to critique popular conceptions of justice in our culture. (Isaiah 1:17; Micah 6:8; Matthew 23:23)

6. **Fruitful Speech:** I commit to engaging in political discourse with speech that is marked by the fruit of the Spirit—love, joy, peace, patience, kindness, goodness, faithfulness, gentleness, self-control. (Galatians 5:22–23; James 3)

7. **Peacemaking:** I commit to face-to-face conflict resolution rather than vitriolic arguments on social media or talking behind someone's back. (Matthew 18:15–17; Romans 12:17–21)

8. **Removing the Log:** I commit to giving more attention to examining the potential flaws in my own political leanings, conduct, and sin than I give to scrutinizing others. (Matthew 7:1–5)

9. **Humble Learning:** I commit to being quick to listen, slow to speak, and slow to anger as I seek to learn from the varied perspectives within the body of Christ. (1 Corinthians 12:12–26; James 1:19)

10. **Loving Enemies:** I commit to loving and praying for my so-called political enemies, especially those I have the hardest time loving and praying for. This includes a commitment to praying for our government leaders regardless of who wins the election. (Matthew 5:43–44; 1 Timothy 2:1–4)

Commitment: During this election season, I commit to following Jesus in my political participation and discourse. While I know that I am a sinner who is imperfect and cannot live out this vision perfectly, I am committed to growing in these ten areas as a means of loving God and my neighbors during these conflicted times.

1. WORSHIP

I commit my allegiance to King Jesus over all idols
and ideologies. (Exodus 20:2–3; Psalm 115:1–8; Philippians 2:9–11)

"They burned down our house," Vinh tells me, "because it was
where our church gathered for worship." Vinh is not angry; he's
actually smiling. We're standing in the rubble of his family's former home. I am in rural Vietnam, visiting a network of underground churches.

Vinh's experience is not uncommon. Many church leaders I
meet with have been jailed or beaten for their faith. They've got
scars to prove it. Persecution has been a reality in this region for
a while now. "Don't pray the persecution ends," they tell me.
"Pray we remain faithful through it."

"How about I pray for both?" I respond, smiling.

Why is their worship seen as a threat? To local authorities, it
signals that their ultimate allegiance lies elsewhere. Don't get
me wrong—they're good citizens. (They believe their commitment to Jesus shapes them to become even *better* citizens.)
And they honor local officials. (They recognize that God has
given the government an important role for the flourishing of
their community.) Yet they also see themselves as citizens of a
greater kingdom, ruled by a higher authority than their government.

Their ultimate allegiance is to the King of kings.

Give your ultimate allegiance to King Jesus. Worship him
over all idols and ideologies. In America, we don't typically
experience persecution, but we do experience pressure. Our
pressure is not to *apostatize* but to *assimilate* to the party plat-

forms and partisan norms of our culture. Too many Christians have succumbed to this pressure and subordinated God to their party.

The antidote is worship. We exalt Christ as King and orient our lives to his kingdom. True worship is not just the songs we sing from our lips but the obedience we give with our lives. "Jesus is Lord"—the central Christian proclamation—is a claim to who is the rightful ruler of the world. The first of God's *actual* Ten Commandments is "Have no other gods before me."[1] That means no idols, no competing allegiances. Rather, we are to "worship the Lord [our] God and serve him only."[2]

The church's prophetic cry should not be "God Bless America" but rather "America Bless God"! It's like when Joshua asked the angel, "Whose side are you on—ours or our enemies'?" and the angel responded, essentially, "Neither, I'm on God's side!"[3] Give him your worship! Ascribe the honor, power, and glory due his name! The right-wing temptation is generally to *subordinate* God to a partisan agenda, slapping him onto a preconceived political religion as if he were a bumper sticker. The left-wing temptation is generally to *marginalize* God from one's political vision, pretending the world runs better off without him. Both are idolatry.

The gospel says no! Jesus is King. The church's rallying cry is not to the four political religions but to the kingdom of God. Worship is a political act; it puts God at the center of our lives in his world. In this respect, we do have something important in common with the church in Vietnam.

Our revolution starts with worship.

2. LOVE OF NEIGHBOR

I commit to participating in civic life as a means of loving and serving my neighbor rather than just serving my own interests. (Matthew 22:34–40; Philippians 2:1–11)

Jim stood face-to-face with a sea of five hundred red-hot angry demonstrators. Chants of "Islam is evil" and "U-S-A" filled the air. Their leader wore a "F*&$ Islam" shirt and claimed that hate speech did not exist. Another protest leader was tearing pages from the Quran and spitting on them. The crowd was waving flags, boasting semiautomatic rifles, and ready for a brawl.

Behind Jim, my friend, was the Islamic Community Center of Phoenix, the object of the angry group's protest. Jim was joined by hundreds of people from our church and other local churches who showed up in support of our Muslim neighbors, forming a wall of solidarity between the demonstrators and their community. The police and FBI had blocked off roads in the surrounding neighborhood and installed security cameras on light posts; helicopters circled overhead. Tensions were high; the threat of violence was real. Protestors called it the "Freedom of Speech Rally."

Jim's side called it the "Love Your Neighbor Rally."

A little background. Earlier that month, two gunmen had opened fire at a "Draw Muhammad" contest in Garland, Texas. (In Islam, physical depictions of Muhammad are considered blasphemous; the two militant extremists were retaliating with violence.) Here in Phoenix, organizers responded by hosting another of the contests, calling protestors to exercise their First Amendment rights ("free speech") by drawing pictures of the prophet near the mosque, and their Second Amendment rights ("bear arms") by bringing their guns to the rally.

Jim saw promotion of the event go viral in Phoenix circles. Through his work with refugees, he had built strong relationships with the Muslim community and wanted them to know they were not alone. So he called up friends and put his own invitation out on social media. Hundreds responded. They wore blue shirts and committed to nonviolence, forming a peaceful line in front of the mosque, facing the protestors. They offered water bottles and friendly conversation to the sea of angry faces before them.

The goal was to be a sign of the gospel. As Jim told a reporter,

> One of the main reasons why we set up here on this sidewalk right now is to create a physical barrier between the mosque and our Muslim friends and potential violence and hostility. . . . So that if they suffer, we suffer with them. To stand in between the potential pain and danger they are in in the same way that Jesus stood in between it for us.[4]

Love is a potent witness. This moment catalyzed more conversations about Jesus with our church's Muslim and non-Christian neighbors than had any other evangelism or outreach program that season.

In a divisive culture, we're called to love our neighbor. Our Muslim neighbor. Our atheist neighbor. Our Democrat or Republican neighbor. Jesus says the greatest command is to love God with all you've got and to "love your neighbor as yourself."[5] That command doesn't go away when the political climate gets hot. When someone asked Jesus, "Who is my neighbor?" (because they wanted an out), the Savior pointed to a Samaritan: a religious other, an ethnic outsider, a political enemy.[6] *That's* your neighbor, Jesus said.

This doesn't mean our differences don't matter. They do. Jim says he wants his Muslim friends to follow Jesus, and they want to convert him, too. Political debate is important; respectful disagreement can be done well. But *how you treat* the neighbor you disagree with matters. Are you willing to love them sacrificially, to put your life on the line for them, the way the good Samaritan did? The way Christ did for you, even when you'd made yourself his enemy?

We can miss the "as yourself" part of Jesus's command to love. He's talking about way more than having good vibes for your neighbor. He's saying that all those things you typically do *for yourself,* get to work creatively using those gifts as instruments of love to also bless others. As the Reformer John Calvin puts it,

> All the gifts we possess have been bestowed by God and entrusted to us on condition that they be distributed for our neighbors' benefit.[7]

In other words, we humans have a propensity to think our time, money, and influence belong to us for our own benefit. The reality is, however, that those things ultimately belong to God. Our responsibility is to steward and leverage those gifts for the sake of those around us. We can use our gifts to throw them a party.

Politics is a means of loving your neighbor. It's not the only way, not even the primary way. But politics is a vehicle for seeking the flourishing of our society. This doesn't solve all the questions about what policies are best; people of good faith will have different opinions and disagree. But our motive should be love.

There's a good gut check here: *Am I motivated by animosity, hatred, or disgust for my political opponent?* If so, then you're being lured away from Christ. Your motive should be love. I'll tell you more about that protest rally in a minute, but the commitment to loving our church's Muslim neighbors built bridges for the gospel in our community.

Every stroke of the pen you use to fill in your ballot, every syllable you spend on a political discussion, every letter you invest in a social media post, and every penny you donate to a political campaign can have the explicit intention of loving God above all else and loving your neighbor as yourself. Each minute of your life is a unit of love God has given to be used for the good of others.

Use it well.

3. IMAGE OF GOD

I commit to honoring the image of God in all people by treating them with respect and abstaining from dehumanizing caricatures. (Genesis 1:26; James 3:9)

Jim says that twenty years ago, he would have been at that anti-Islam rally. After 9/11, he was angry. "I bought into dehumanizing caricatures," he states, "that painted all my Muslim neighbors with the same broad brushstrokes of radical extremism." In his circles, some people blamed them for the attack. There was a lot of hostility and a desire for action, with people using coarse language and misrepresentation to incite others against them.[8]

Some friends challenged Jim, however. He was a newer Christian, so they pulled him aside, opened the Scriptures, and explained, "This way of talking and acting is inconsistent with who Jesus is." It shook him and started him on a journey to discovering what it really looks like to treat his Muslim neighbor as someone who bears the image of God. This eventually led him to serve as a missionary in Turkey.

The book of James confronts us, like Jim's friends sitting him down to challenge him, about how "we praise our Lord and Father, and with [that same mouth] we curse human beings, who have been made in God's likeness."[9] James is saying there's a link between how we speak about God and how we speak about humans. Just like we can't mock a painting while claiming to respect the artist, we can't mock an image bearer while claiming to honor their Creator.

When we make fun of people with different political leanings, it's often because we've stopped seeing them as humans and started seeing them as caricatures. Many today write off left-leaning folks as "social justice warriors," or right-leaning folks as "white racist bigots." One church member, Heather, cares deeply about unborn lives and works at a crisis-pregnancy center, but many dismiss her, saying she's just another Karen who wants to turn America into *The Handmaid's Tale*. Another, Alex, grew up in America but is undocumented and working for immigration reform, yet many dismiss him, saying he's just a woke millennial who wants everything handed to him without having to work for it.

When we misrepresent people like this, we are refusing to take their concerns seriously. It's lazy. James tells us it's disrespectful to treat people like they are not "made in the likeness of God."[10] It's all too common in our culture but should not be so for Christ followers.

Maybe you've never insulted God directly, but when you insult humans, you actually *are* insulting God. You're ridiculing the pinnacle of his creation, whom he loves and died for. That's ridiculous for a true worshipper, James goes on to explain, like fresh water and salt water both flowing from the same spring, or a fig tree producing olives.[11] Worship of God should flow out in respect for his image bearers. When your roots are in Jesus, your fruit should be love.

When you approach someone as an image bearer rather than a caricature, you show up with attentiveness, respect, and a sincere posture of listening. As theologian Vincent Bacote says, we are "to have fidelity to God expressed as respect for others."[12] You can (and probably will) still disagree, but I guarantee you'll have much better conversations.

The "image of God" gives us a category for how we treat everybody, regardless of their political or religious affiliation. In the years since Jim was confronted about his anti-Muslim sentiments, he has made strong, close friendships with a number of Muslim people. He says they've literally saved his and his wife's lives several times. For example, there was Dr. Ebru, who answered her personal cellphone in the middle of the night to rescue his wife with an emergency surgery. Or Emre, who recognized that Jim and his wife had a carbon monoxide leak in their home and offered to host the young Christian couple in his country. They disagree about Jesus, and that's vitally important, but he treats them with respect. He invites them into his home; they have great party conversations. He speaks to them and about them as those created in the image and likeness of God.

Because they are.

4. BIBLICAL WISDOM

I commit to having my views challenged by the biblical story rather than using the Bible to proof-text my predetermined positions. (Psalm 119; 2 Timothy 3:16)

Rachel and her friends brought explosives to a protest in downtown Phoenix and were planning to incite violence, but they got caught and were then arrested. Rachel believed she was fighting for justice. That past year, she had also changed her pronouns, had begun taking testosterone, and was on her way toward sex-reassignment surgery. She was advocating for legal changes to punish parents who didn't support their children's transitioning. Rachel worshipped in the Religion of Identity.

Rachel was also exploring Jesus, however. She joined a group I was leading, with an openness to letting the biblical story challenge her understanding of both justice and gender. She was invited to encounter God's perspective on the matters she cared most deeply about.

We need God's Word to challenge our deepest-held views and cultural assumptions rather than to simply use God as an appendage to our preexisting political commitments. If you're going to resist the ideologies of our culture, you need to immerse yourself in the biblical story.

We're surrounded by false stories in our culture. They seek to form our allegiance to the idols, narrating our lives around what they offer. The story of self-expressive individualism (discussed in chapter 1), for example, had heavily shaped Rachel's approach to both justice and gender and cultivated in her an allegiance to the idol of identity. She's not alone.[13]

We're all shaped by a story, whether we realize it or not. While these stories often originate in a long history of philosophical thought that we're unaware of, they nonetheless seep into our minds through the clichés of friends, the allure of advertisements, pep talks from coaches, our favorite songs and tear-jerking movies, talking heads on the news, and our seemingly simple habits that reinforce the narratives in our lives.

How can you know if you're being shaped by the biblical story more than by propaganda for idols? Here are a few questions to ask. First, *Does God's perspective ever disagree with my political leanings?* If the Bible seems to perfectly align with your politics, then you're either the first person in history not to struggle with idolatry or you're subconsciously editing the Bible to make it more palatable to your preferences.

Don't be like Thomas Jefferson, who famously cut out any reference to miracles in his Bible. Don't edit God's story to fit your political religion; edit your allegiance to align with God's story.

Allow the Bible to challenge you.

A second question to ask: *What sources of information dominate my time and attention?* You can fill your days with podcasts and pundits, tweets from political influencers, videos from favorite commentators, and your preferred cable news network running eternally in the background.

These are not just streams of political information; they become sacred texts aimed at our formation. They move our hearts, shape our conversations, occupy our minds, and narrate the story we're living within. We can be deceived into thinking our political opinions are simply the rational product of our own personal reflection, when we're actually following an idolatrous script that's being narrated to us, driving forward a story that will ultimately fail us and harm the world in the process.[14] We can wind up celebrating the wrong things, like a drunken party animal belligerently wreaking havoc against God's kingdom.

So, how healthy is your information diet? "Blessed is the one," the psalmist proclaimed, "whose delight is in the [instruction] of the LORD, and who meditates on his law day and night."[15] We need to soak in the true story of the King and his kingdom, allowing his truth to shape our hearts, minds, and lives. Our discipleship involves learning to approach all of life—work, family, rest, civic engagement, and more—through the lens of his grand, redemptive story.

Read the news, but submit to the Word of God.

5. BIBLICAL JUSTICE

I commit to understanding and pursuing justice as I engage in civic life, not minimizing Scripture's repeated call to seek justice, and allowing Scripture to critique popular conceptions of justice in our culture. (Isaiah 1:17; Micah 6:8; Matthew 23:23)

"That Mexican Jew keeps talking about justice." Ashley explained why she was leaving our church. I am Mexican. (Not much I can do about that!) I'm not Jewish, but Jesus is. (So if you have a problem with that, you're going to have to take it up with him.) But what about her concern that I talk too much about justice? While I don't think I spend an inordinate amount of time talking about it, we pastors do preach through books of the Bible and the topic comes up regularly.

Ashley worships in the Religion of Security. The rest of her email made that clear. And she was voicing a concern that's become increasingly frequent in many circles: that any talk of justice is veiled Marxist dogma. *Be wary if your pastor starts talking about social justice,* some prominent church leaders have warned. *It's the devil's doctrine in disguise.*

Now, there are unhealthy versions of justice out there. (I've seen some of the crazy postmodern versions; they're definitely alive and well.)[16] So we do need to allow Scripture to critique some popular versions of justice in our culture.

But here's the thing: While not every version of social justice is biblical, biblical justice is always social.

Justice is *everywhere* in Scripture. The primary terms for justice appear more than seven hundred times.[17] For context, that's more often than the terms for money, sex, and prayer appear (though, obviously, justice relates to all three). God is a "mighty King, lover of justice"[18] who regularly commands his people to "do justice," not just virtue signal about it. Even beyond the terms, you can hardly turn a page without coming across the concept. So, in regards to Ashley's concern, I wonder if I've talked about justice enough—I'm not quite keeping up with God.

Biblical justice is driven by the love of God as an expression of worship. And it's oriented toward the good of your neighbor and the flourishing of society. In other words, it's *social*.

That is why we must commit to pursuing justice in civic life: God commands it. Don't shy away from talking about justice because you're worried someone might call you a Marxist. Don't minimize Scripture's repeated call to seek justice because people like Ashley might leave your church. God is a God of justice, which is good news for a world desperately in need of being put right.

The best defense is a good offense. The best response to *bad* visions of justice in our society is not *no* vision of justice but a *good* vision of justice. It's God's vision of justice. Don't let the devil steal the good terms; reclaim them. We need to be talking *more* about justice in our churches, not less.

We don't need edited Bibles. Don't be like the slaveholders whose infamous "slave Bibles" edited out the Exodus and the many references to freedom for slaves. Slaves needed the *whole* Bible, not parts—and so do the oppressed today. Slave owners needed the whole Bible too—they needed to be confronted by God the way Pharaoh was—and so do we.

You have a slaveholder's Bible if you ignore or reimagine the parts dealing with God's heart for justice because you're afraid it will get you called a Marxist. Or if you edit out and revise the parts dealing with sexuality because it sounds prudish and you want to sleep around. Or if you push away the parts dealing with the power of the Holy Spirit because you can rely on your own strength without that "ancient superstition." Or if you cut out the parts dealing with forgiveness because *others just don't know what they've done.*

As Augustine famously observed, if you believe what you like in the gospel, and reject what you don't like, it is not the gospel you believe, but yourself.[19]

We need the whole God of the whole Bible. As theologian A. J. Swoboda notes, "The real tool of oppression was a deconstructed, redacted, and edited Bible. . . . The institution of slavery didn't end because people stopped reading the Bible. The institution of slavery started to end because people finally started reading the whole Bible."[20] We need to read the whole Bible too—including its repeated call to justice—and start taking it seriously.

Doing so will draw us near to the heart of God.

6. FRUITFUL SPEECH

I commit to engaging in political discourse with speech that's marked by the fruit of the Spirit—love, joy, peace, patience, kindness, goodness, faithfulness, gentleness, self-control. (Galatians 5:22–23; James 3)

If I told you I had a cherry tree but come springtime there were apples bursting off its branches, you'd probably be suspicious. You would think, *Apples don't come from cherry trees.* Exactly. Jesus warns of people who use his name but aren't really of him, saying, "You will know them by their [fruit]."²¹ Some people claim to be "Jesus trees," but their fruit says otherwise.

So, what fruit do Jesus trees bear? Paul gave nine in his classic list: "The fruit of the Spirit is love, joy, peace, patience, kindness, goodness, faithfulness, gentleness, self-control."²² We're called to such character, and there's no political-exemption clause. What might such fruit look like in the political arena?

Love: Can you imagine someone walking away from a political disagreement feeling loved? I've had many intense conversations with Jim, my friend mentioned earlier in this chapter, but I always feel cared for by him. He listens charitably and is more interested in God's glory than his own. Even a rebuke from him feels more loving than a compliment from others because I know he wants my good. What if others walked away from you having the same experience in heated cultural conversations?

Joy: What if our social media posts celebrated what we are for more than what we are against? If we publicly named what we appreciate about our political opponents—even amid deep disagreement? If we spoke against injustice *and* celebrated the benefits of good policy—even when accomplished by the "other side"? It may seem a bit Pollyannaish to send more thank-you cards than hate mail, but it's actually a Christian celebration of common grace. You don't have to choose between celebrating the good and challenging evil. Joyful gratitude can do both.

Peace: What if we maintained a non-anxious presence amid a cultural storm? We can when we're rooted in God's peace. We don't need to process every emotion online or go into every conversation with defenses up. We were reconciled to God while still his enemies, so we should be the first when conflict arises to admit wrong, confess sin, and extend forgiveness.

Patience: What if we slowed down and listened well? Not feeling the pressure to rush a response or give a hot take? We don't have to interrupt, dreaming up that powerful one-liner before the other person has finished speaking. We can ask good questions, taking our time to really consider what the other person is saying before drawing conclusions. Sometimes we might even try mentally taking their position and trying to defend it (like they taught us on debate team) as a means of exploring others' logic and thinking.

Kindness: What if politicians running for office posted things they liked about their opponent? (That would surprise their base!) Keep your heart pure and your hands clean. You can be direct, say what you really think—and still be polite and respectful.

Goodness: What if you gave your annoying uncle a pass at Thanksgiving dinner? Take the high road. Do not repay evil for evil, but overcome evil with good.[23] Make sure you're still able to kiss your mom with that mouth and praise your heavenly Father with it too.

Faithfulness: What if we refused to be people pleasers who capitulated to the various ideologies of our day? What if we honored Jesus with faithful witness? Conservative Christians would challenge greed, even if it meant family and friends might call them socialists. Progressive Christians would lament the horror of abortion, even if it meant being ostracized in their circles.

Gentleness: Imagine a church marked by wise and measured words. Leaders would refuse to engage in vitriolic rants to build platforms and gain followers in the culture wars. Followers would refuse to divide their churches by planting a flag in one of the political religions. *Gentle* can sound weak in our culture, but

Jesus describes himself as "gentle and lowly in heart."[24] As Dane C. Ortlund puts it, that means Jesus is

> meek. Humble. Gentle. Jesus is not trigger-happy. Not harsh, reactionary, easily exasperated. He is the most understanding person in the universe. The posture most natural to him is not a pointed finger but open arms.[25]

Jesus is gentle toward us and helps us extend that to others. Let's exchange bitterness for gentleness, get rid of the trigger-happy pointed finger of the Right and the Left, to adopt the posture of Jesus.

Self-Control: What if you hit pause before sending that text message? Or didn't post that comment to Facebook? Or slept on that email before sending it? The Spirit can empower you to not say things you'll later wish you could take back. You can't reel them back in! Self-control can help you refrain from using harsh and unproductive words.

So, that's what it means to be a Jesus tree, with his Spirit flowing through your branches. If you say you're an oak of righteousness planted in God's lovely garden but you're bursting with animosity, bitterness, cynicism, and pride, people will rightly say, "I didn't think that grew on Jesus's trees." *Exactly.*

Jesus's better party is serving the fruit of the Spirit.

* * *

Okay, the final four commitments all have to do with peacemaking. This is a significant topic all its own, so the whole next chapter is devoted to it.

Reflection Questions

- Which of the six commitments in this chapter is easiest for you to embrace? Why? Thank God for the way he's at work in your life.

- Which of the six commitments is most challenging for you? Ask God what it would look like to press into that commitment.

- In what ways can you ensure that your views are challenged by the biblical story rather than using the Bible to proof-text your predetermined positions?

- Audit your language: Think about the ways you speak about those who lean toward different quadrants. Does the way you speak about them portray a conviction that they are made in God's image and worthy of your respect?

- Identify someone with whom you disagree strongly about politics. How might you interact more charitably and kindly the next time you see this person?

BREAKERS, FAKERS, AND MAKERS

"Why do you want to get rid of all borders?" Mike asked. A.J., one of our church leaders, was shocked by the question. He'd never said anything of the sort.

When Mike invited him to lunch, A.J. was unaware it was an intervention. A.J. suggested his favorite restaurant (ironically, one owned by Palestinian refugees). Mike arrived incredulous, wanting to challenge some things A.J. (supposedly) had said about immigration.

"Where did you hear that?" A.J. asked. Turns out, someone attended a class he'd taught six months prior at our church. They had shared A.J.'s (alleged) statement with a handful of people—including Mike. The comment had really angered them all. Here was A.J., one of their leaders, advocating for policies they found ridiculous and harmful. This was an abuse of his position, they reasoned. For months, they discussed it together, reading articles and preparing arguments for why A.J. was wrong. Now Mike was here to represent this group and set him straight.

There was conflict; they needed peace.

How should A.J. respond? Is there anything Mike should have done differently? How do we deal with such conflict in a Jesus-shaped way?

Before I share what happened, I want to use this as a case study for peacemaking. Conflict over politics is tearing the church apart—alienating friendships, fracturing families, and dividing congregations. We need practical tools for addressing such conflict. We've already explored the first six of our Ten Political Commandments. We'll now deal with the final four, which all have to do with peacemaking.[1]

When you hear the word *peace*, what image first comes to mind? Perhaps it's

- *a hippie in tie-dye waving a peace sign.* They're smiling and wishing you "Good vibes, man!" but strike you as naïve. Peace here is wishful thinking with no real power to change the world.

- *United Nations peacekeepers with blue helmets in a conflict zone.* Here peace is the work of diplomats and political leaders who negotiate treaties and build barricades. Important stuff, but not relevant to most of us.

- *incense, yoga, and chamomile tea.* Peace here is "inner peace," trying to shut out the world with lavender, essential oils, a battery-powered babbling brook, magnesium supplements, and meditation apps. Calm and relaxing, perhaps, but not community building.

Peace is either way "out there" or way "in here" in each of these examples. So some of us understandably roll our eyes when we hear the word *peace*. It seems impractical to our everyday lives. Such peace is unable to speak to the aforementioned conflict over immigration.

Yet God's vision for peace is *way* more practical—and way

more vital for the political mess we're in today—than you might think. Peace is the atmosphere of God's kingdom party. Let's start with *why* we should be committed to peacemaking in the first place.

GOD OF PEACE

God is called the God of Peace more than ten times in Scripture.[2] So peacemaking is not just something God does; it's *who God is.* Jesus is the "Prince of Peace."[3] That means it's in his job description. If Jesus handed you his business card, *peacemaker* would be on it. "He himself is our peace," Paul declared, "who has made the two groups one and has destroyed the barrier, the dividing wall of hostility."[4] Christ has made peace through his cross.

Peacemaking is central to the gospel.

It is not a hobby for Jesus, like someone who occasionally snowboards in the winter. It's not a side hustle the Savior does to make extra cash. No, it's one of his main things.

What is this peace? The Hebrew word is *shalom,* which entails much more than just the absence of conflict. It involves the presence of flourishing in our relationships with God, ourselves, others, and the broader creation. As theologian Cornelius Plantinga puts it,

> The webbing together of God, humans, and all creation in justice, fulfillment, and delight is what the Hebrew prophets call *shalom.* We call it peace, but it means far more than mere peace of mind or cease-fire between enemies. In the Bible, shalom means *universal flourishing, wholeness, and delight*—a rich state of affairs in which natural needs are satisfied and natural gifts fruitfully employed, a state of

affairs that inspires joyful wonder as its Creator and Savior opens doors and welcomes the creatures in whom he delights. Shalom, in other words, is the way things ought to be.[5]

That is the party that creation was made for. God is out to re-web these relationships. That's what the gospel is all about. "God was pleased to have all his fullness dwell in [Jesus]," Colossians tells us, "to reconcile to himself all things, whether things on earth or things in heaven, by *making peace* through his blood, shed on the cross."[6] That's the goal of the Cross. To reconcile fractured relationships. All of them. In heaven and on earth. To restore shalom. To make peace.

The God of Peace is on a peacemaking mission.

This is important. If we're going to care about peace, we must see how central it is to the heart of God. If A.J. was not just going to write Mike off, he needed to recognize that God was out to re-web their relationship. Making peace is not just a *good* thing to do; it's a *God* thing to do.

"Blessed are the peacemakers," Jesus says, "for they will be called children of God."[7] God is calling you into the family business. As a child of God, you're called to join your heavenly Father and Christ, his Son, on their peacemaking mission to the world. God has entrusted you with his "[gospel] of peace" and his "ministry of reconciliation."[8] Jesus breathes his Spirit of peace upon us to empower us in this mission.[9] You're called to restore broken relationships. To actively pursue shalom. To rebuild a broken world. To bring back the party that creation was made for.

That is why our church's seventh commitment is peacemaking.

7. PEACEMAKING

I commit to face-to-face conflict resolution rather than vitriolic arguments on social media or talking behind someone's back. (Matthew 18:15–17; Romans 12:17–21)

With Mike, one challenge was that his small group had been talking about A.J. for months behind his back. A quick phone call or in-person chat in passing could have saved months of time and energy. "Hey, A.J., I heard you said this. Is that true?" "No, I actually said this." "Oh, okay! Thanks. Bye." I've found that so many conflicts could easily be resolved if we just went directly to the person and asked for clarification.

Before you think A.J.'s the hero of this story, however, he shared that he did the same thing.

"I actually knew this group was talking about me. Someone told me. The person went on to accuse this whole group of thinking all immigrants were rapists and terrorists. I'm ashamed to say that rather than reaching out to Mike or this group to clarify, I began subtly gossiping about them to others. I started looking up statistics to build my argument against them."

Yet A.J. and the group saw one another regularly. They were involved in various ministries together and smiled as they crossed paths over several months. They answered day-to-day mundane questions, nodding in affirmation as if nothing was wrong. They ignored the unspoken tension between them.

This was peacefaking.

Peacefaking is when you avoid conflict and ignore tension. You smile and pretend everything's all right. Either you're afraid to address the issue or you don't want to take the time, so you fake it. Are you peacefaking in any relationships? Are you ignoring the lumps in the carpet of your friendship, pretending every-thing's okay in order to keep the peace?

Peacefaking is not peacemaking. Sadly, many confuse the two, but they're not the same thing. Peacefaking is actually one of the biggest enemies to peacemaking because we use it to jus-tify our apathy. We say we're just "keeping the peace," but it al-lows animosity to fester. It's a failure to love.

Jesus didn't call you to be a peace*keeper* but a peace*maker*. Sure, there's a time to overlook an offense and let it go. But if you find resentment building or a desire to gossip about and slander the person, that's a sign to stop being a peacefaker and become a peacemaker.

So, how do we do that? How did A.J. make peace with Mike? How do we handle conflict well? We've developed four steps at our church. The first is to get with God.

GET WITH GOD

Hard conversations often fail because we fail to prepare. We don't bring the issue to God and ask him to search our hearts and reveal our motives. Jesus speaks to the importance of deal-ing with one's own heart first before addressing an issue with another person:

> How can you say to your brother, "Let me take the speck [of sawdust] out of your eye," when there is the log in your own eye? You hypocrite, first take the log out of your own eye, and then you will see clearly to take the speck out of your brother's eye.[10]

That is a call to slow down and prepare before having a hard conversation. Jesus calls us to self-reflection: I need to audit my own actions, motives, and potential sin before I address the problems of others. A.J. said that before putting Mike under a microscope, he needed to look at himself in the mirror.

Jesus's teaching is brilliant. (He knows his stuff!) If both parties were ruthlessly dedicated to discovering and dealing with their own issues, how much conflict could be easily resolved? This would solve most roommate tensions, marital arguments, and church controversies and probably a good share of international conflicts. It would keep the Enemy from crashing Jesus's kingdom party.

This brings us to our eighth commitment.

8. REMOVING THE LOG

I commit to giving more attention to critiquing the potential flaws in my own political leanings, conduct, and sin than I give to scrutinizing others. (Matthew 7:1–5)

The goal here is to ask, *Is there a way I've been a peacebreaker? How have I possibly contributed to the problem or tension between us?* To join Jesus as peacemakers, we need to not only stop being peacefakers but also own the ways we've been peacebreakers.

The problem is that we live in a world where we rarely admit we're wrong. We've all become experts who scrutinize the flaws of others with a microscope, yet we are often blind to the areas where we need to grow. Admitting a mistake or even a wrong opinion is often seen as weak. Yet this prideful posture prevents peace. If everyone says, "I'm definitely right," the community will implode. A willingness to say, "I might be wrong," can help the church thrive.

Now, to be clear, this doesn't necessarily mean you are the one who objectively carries the most fault. But it does mean we need to view the issues on our side of the line with the highest degree of seriousness and scrutiny.

The following are questions that can be helpful to ask when preparing for a hard conversation (using the answers A.J. gave, with his permission, as an example):

- *What are my motives?* With Mike, was my goal to prove him wrong and take him down or to truly seek clarity and understanding?

- *What do I need to repent of?* I had to own up, before God, to ways I had gossiped about Mike to others.

- *Where might I be misunderstanding?* Was it possible that Mike's group had been misrepresented and there was more to the story?

- *What story am I telling myself?* I asked myself if it was true that Mike was a racist. Or was I using that label to write him off rather than engage him well?

- *Are there idols or ideologies influencing my perspective?* I wanted to examine my own quadrant's political leanings and how it might be influencing my perception of Mike.

- *What are my emotions?* I had to acknowledge there was some anger and bitterness. Naming this and bringing it before God was helpful for defusing it and being self-aware going into the conversation.

- *How can I seek appropriate counsel without gossip or slander?* I found one trusted person (not a bigger group) who was mature enough to help me process the situation without disparaging Mike.

- *What is the specific issue I want to bring up?* I've found it best to focus on one issue at a time, so I unbundled other issues I had with Mike to save them for a different conversation.

- *What would it look like to forgive the other person? Can I overlook this offense, or will there be ongoing tension I need to resolve? What are my expectations of this person? Are they biblical? What would this person need to own for reconciliation to be possible? What hopes do I have for this conversation on the other side?*

Many hard conversations spin out of control because we go into them without going to God first. Conflicts often dissipate once we realize that we have overstated the other person's issue and overlooked our own sinful issues. So many relationships could be spared if we brought such questions to God initially in a posture of humble self-reflection and were prepared to enter the hard conversation well.

* * *

I'll share what happened next with A.J. and Mike in a moment, but Jesus's wisdom applies to political conflict more broadly. Beyond one-on-one relationships, it can heal how we approach those in other political quadrants. It can keep us from becoming political armchair quarterbacks.

Have you ever found yourself yelling at the TV, "Move faster, you lazy bum!"? I can criticize the speed of Kyler Murray, one of the fastest quarterbacks in the NFL, while balancing a plate of nachos on my chest (so it's closer to my mouth) and not having moved from my couch in an hour. The irony is, he could run for a 97-yard touchdown before I refilled my plate of nachos.

I'm an armchair quarterback, and I'm not alone. Every fall,

millions of accountants, schoolteachers, construction workers, and pastors are magically transformed into football experts. We yell at the TV: "You just need to run the ball!" We critique the players: "He needs to develop his footwork." As if there were a direct line from our living rooms to the little headsets worn by coaches.

This armchair-quarterback mentality might be harmless while watching football, but it's dangerous when it comes to politics. We're often experts at evaluating the shortcomings of other camps while blind to our own camp's weaknesses and failures. I must confess, when it comes to politics, I often show up with a microscope in hand to look for the flaws of those in other camps while being slow to pull out a mirror and examine my own. Jesus says to pay more attention to your own shortcomings than to the flaws of others. This applies to your political leanings as well.

Don't be a political armchair quarterback.

We should be wary of fake boldness. It's where Christians will claim to speak boldly on some social issue when it's really something their circle already agrees on. Perhaps this is the conservative-leaning congregation deep in the suburbs with an older demographic that regularly lambasts critical race theory. Or the progressive-leaning congregation in the urban core with a younger demographic that regularly lambasts Christian nationalism. Each knows it tickles the ears of their audience. While touted as boldness, this can ignore the temptations in one's own community. It can fire a warning shot at an idol across town while providing safety under a cover of distraction for the idol in their midst.

Now, to be clear, this doesn't mean we should not challenge sin, idolatry, and injustice promoted by others. It merely means we put ourselves and our camp in front of the mirror first. Real courage involves taking a bold look in the mirror at our own lives and churches, to honestly name what we see. It's those who lean toward

- *the Religion of Progress:* being the first to name the damage done in the name of science, including surging rates of anxiety, depression, and suicide for younger generations addicted to social media.

- *the Religion of Responsibility:* identifying the oppression and injustice many people endure through no fault of their own, while helping to remove obstacles for the downtrodden to succeed in a thriving society.

- *the Religion of Identity:* honestly assessing the infertility and irreparable damage many young people will face later as adults after being cheered into hormone therapy and sex reassignment surgeries.

- *the Religion of Security:* recognizing the need for strong institutions and lamenting the dangers of an "Us versus Them" mentality, while working hard to debunk anti-immigrant misinformation and open their homes to refugees.

Few things would be more powerful than a church that takes Jesus's teaching seriously, one in which we put a higher priority—as both individuals and a group—on addressing our own conduct and the idols in our own camp.

Owning our "logs" will better position us to address the "speck" in our brothers and sisters. We won't agree on every policy—that's okay. But we can agree that Jesus is serious when he calls us to stop being armchair quarterbacks and start training ourselves for the game.

GET TOGETHER

After you get with God, the next step is to get together. Now that you've removed the log from your own eye, you're ready to address the speck in your brother's eye. Conflicts often grow because we ignore Jesus's words to directly address the issue one-on-one with the hope of being peacemakers. Jesus tells us,

> If your brother sins against you, go and tell him his fault, between you and him alone. If he listens to you, you have gained your brother.[11]

Jesus tells us to go talk to the person. Instead, we're often tempted to talk *about* the person behind their back. We ignore Jesus's command to "go and tell him his fault" and instead go to *others* to tell *them* his fault. Mike and A.J. realized they disobeyed Jesus when they gossiped about each other, damaging their reputations with other people in our church, which they later had to go back and repair. Don't gossip and slander; it's destructive. It can ruin reputations and divide communities. Scripture is replete with such warnings.[12]

Don't talk *about* the person; talk *to* the person.

With that said, if you're in an abusive or dangerous situation, that's different. Use wisdom. It may not be safe to meet with the person one-on-one. Getting help in such situations is not gossip; it's obtaining the support you need to get safe or confront such sinful patterns.[13]

We're also tempted to lambast the person publicly on social media. This ignores Jesus's command to address the issue "between you and him alone." Don't misunderstand me—it's fine to disagree publicly and debate on social media. But if you find yourself feeling mean-spirited and posting vitriolic comments on someone's feed because of a conflict or tension, take it offline. Hop on the phone or grab coffee together to hash it out privately without a crowd of blood-lusting spectators cheering on your gladiator match in the internet colosseum. Don't contribute to that bad party.

That is countercultural these days but worth doing. So much is lost when we talk only via text without being able to see the other person's face and hear their voice. It's an important discipline to make an effort to talk in person or at least over the phone or even FaceTime.

Jesus says the hope is to "[gain] your brother." The goal is not taking them down but winning them back. In other words, it's peacemaking. That means entering the conversation with a posture of humble learning, the ninth commitment.

9. HUMBLE LEARNING

I commit to being quick to listen, slow to speak, and slow to anger as I seek to learn from the varied perspectives within the body of Christ. (1 Corinthians 12:12–26; James 1:19)

When Mike and A.J. got together, they discovered that their conflict was largely based on a misunderstanding. As they talked, Mike learned that A.J. never actually said we should get rid of borders. He simply said there are more than twenty million refugees in the world who have suffered profoundly, that God cares greatly for those who suffer, and that God calls us as his people to care for refugees and immigrants who are in our city.[14]

A.J. was even careful to say in the class that he's not attempting to define what our nation's best immigration policy should be (which is debatable) but is addressing the church's responsibility to care for those immigrants who *are* here (which is nonnegotiable). Mike agreed with this.

Months of unspoken relational tension could have been avoided with a simple conversation. James tells us to be "quick to listen, slow to speak and slow to become angry."[15] Mike and his friends inverted this: They were slow to listen, taking six months before asking A.J. to clarify. They were quick to speak— Mike owned up to his group's connecting A.J.'s statement to a Breitbart article they read and gossiping about him to one another. They were quick to get angry.

Tragically, all this happened over something A.J. never said.

A.J. also owned the ways he had misrepresented the group. The irony is, when they finally sat down to talk, they discovered their beliefs weren't all that different. Once they talked face-to-face, it was easy for A.J. to explain that he didn't think we should get rid of borders and for Mike to explain that he didn't think all immigrants were rapists and terrorists. They both believed that Christians should care for refugees and that there should be an orderly process to legally enter the United States.

They had a lot of the same core beliefs but came at them from different angles. Mike wanted to love his neighbors by making sure there was a good process to vet people coming across the borders and keep our country safe. A.J. wanted to love our refugee neighbors, who had endured incredible suffering, by calling us as Christians to embrace them with the hospitality of God and welcome them with friendship to our city.

They both discovered they had bolstered their arguments with bad information. Mike claimed the crime rate was much higher among refugees; A.J. claimed a refugee has never been involved with terrorism. However, when they looked into it, Mike was wrong about the crime rate of refugees, and A.J. was wrong about refugees never attempting terrorism.[16]

Through listening, they both learned from each other.

We need more listening. We need to assume the best of one another rather than jumping to conclusions. You can build strong friendships with people from different persuasions, learning from their leaning, and gleaning from their perspective. Here are a few tips for approaching a hard conversation with a posture of humble learning:

- *Open with an honest confession.* If you have anything to own in the conflict, lead with that. Even if you feel the other person is 90 percent in the wrong and you're only 10 percent responsible, opening vulnerably with your 10 percent will bring their defenses down and pave the way for a fruitful conversation.

- *Use questions rather than accusations.* Rather than accusing A.J., Mike could have said, "I heard you claimed we should get rid of all borders. Is that true? If so, what did you mean by that?" Such questions suggest a posture of humble learning and bring the defenses down, inviting conversation.

- *Speak the truth in love.* Let the person know how their actions hurt you or affected you. Be honest. Be clear. I find it helpful to prepare a sentence or two summarizing the core issue that I'm hoping for them to own or explain.

- *Use God-honoring speech.* Your words matter. This is where getting with God beforehand can help prepare your heart to not unnecessarily enflame or exacerbate the conflict with hasty words you'll later regret but rather to use fruitful speech in the Spirit of Christ that is both honest and loving.

- *Grant forgiveness.* If the person owns their sin, mistake, or mistreatment of you, forgive them as Christ forgave you. (If they don't own it, we'll address that in a minute.) Meeting with God beforehand helps here too; it is the power of receiving his forgiveness toward us that empowers us to forgive others.

- *Make things right.* Mike and A.J. went back to the people they gossiped with to own their mistake in an attempt to repair each other's reputation. Examine if there's any work you need to do to help make amends in the aftermath of reconciliation.

* * *

Mike and A.J. restored their relationship. They've since reaped the benefits of a fruitful friendship, shutting down slander, preventing possible division from crashing our church community, and knowing each other not as political enemies but as brothers in Christ. Jesus's way works.

However, what do you do if the person refuses to own their sin or if the situation only gets worse? Jesus provides the answer:

> If he does not listen, take one or two others along with you, that every charge may be established by the evidence of two or three witnesses.[17]

This is not about finding another person who is on your side in order to win an argument; it's about helping both parties see reality. You can think of this person as either a *witness* (a second pair of eyes), a *mediator* (an impartial referee), or an *arbitrator* (a decision-maker). This final category is usually someone with an authoritative voice, such as a manager, outside expert, elder within a church, or parent within a home.

Good intentions can have bad results if we don't follow God's process. We will experience the spread of gossip, the division that results from sin, and the erosion of trust and relationship. In sum, God's process (so far) involves these steps:

1. Get with God.
2. Get together.
3. Get help.

But there's one last step, which is the heart behind this whole process.

GIVE THE GOSPEL

Being a peacemaker is more than a nice thing to do; it's a way to give the gospel. To extend what we have received. To pay forward what we've been given in Christ. To welcome people to the party, even when they might not deserve it.

"While we were still sinners," Paul said, "Christ died for us." That's how serious Jesus takes peacemaking: He's willing to give his life for it. "We were reconciled to God," Paul continued, "by the death of his Son."[18] That's how serious God the Father takes peacemaking: He's willing to give his Son for it. "The punishment that brought us peace was on him."[19] That's how far God is willing to go to make peace: to hell and back.

Peacemaking is God's family business. The Father and Son undertake this work together in the power of their Spirit. We're invited into their family business. As children of God, we're called to join the triune God in pursuing peace. "As far as it depends on you," the apostle said, "live at peace with everyone."[20]

We're called to be a people of peace as children of the God of Peace.

This isn't about the UN peacekeepers with the blue helmets, because God isn't just about *keeping* the peace; he's about *making* peace. This isn't the naive wishful thinking of a hippie with good vibes, because it's the hard work of a bloody cross in the rocky soil of our war-torn world. This isn't the inner peace of incense and chamomile tea, because it's reconciling former enemies into a community of newly minted friends.

God's peace has grit.

Peacemaking isn't just a hobby for the church; it is core to our job description. That brings us to our tenth and final commitment.

10. LOVING ENEMIES

I commit to loving and praying for my so-called political enemies, especially those I have the hardest time loving and praying for. This includes a commitment to praying for our government leaders regardless of who wins the election. (Matthew 5:43–44; 1 Timothy 2:1–4)

Loving our enemies is hard! What do we do when we don't want to? When we're too hurt, bitter, or cynical? Where will we find the resources for that kind of love?

We need to turn to Jesus! When peacemaking is hard, the plan is not to try harder but rather to dive deeper. Dive deeper into what the Prince of Peace has done for you. Those who have been forgiven much, Jesus says, love much.[21] So, if you're struggling to forgive, plunge into the depths of how much you've been forgiven. If you're lacking love, soak in the reality of God's great love for you. If you find yourself not wanting to move toward others, dive deeper into the reality that Jesus moved toward you.

Before we can give the gospel, we must receive it. Before we can *extend* forgiveness to others, we must *embrace* our own forgiveness in Christ. Jesus is not only our *inspiration* as a distant example but our *motivation* as our personal Great Redeemer. Our heavenly Father's reconciling embrace is where we find the strength for the hard work of peacemaking.

The courage to join God's family business is found in God.

God's reputation is on the line, however, so this work is serious. Any father who invites his children into the family business is taking a risk, because, like it or not, his reputation is linked to the work of his children. Our primary relationship with God is as children, not employees, but being his children means we're enlisted in the family business of loving enemies and making peace. When we refuse to live into our job description as the church, it's God who gets the bad Yelp review, not just us.

When my friend David was a kid, his mom gave him a job. She worked in real estate and asked him to pass out flyers for her agency. She promised to pay him ten cents for every flyer he handed out. He realized he could game the system, however, and dump the stack of flyers in a trash can, go eat ice cream at Dairy Queen, and cash out a few hours later. She'd never know!

While David was devouring his Blizzard, a massive haboob (one of the big dust storms we get in Phoenix) blew through town. It knocked the trash can over and blew his mom's flyers all over that nice, ritzy neighborhood (where people really cared about their yards). His mom received dozens of phone calls from angry neighbors saying they would *never* use her business.

David had tarnished her reputation. She worked hard, did a great job, and commissioned him to represent her. Yet his poor behavior harmed her standing in the neighborhood.

Similarly, when we don't take peacemaking seriously, we tarnish God's reputation. God has given us the gift of peace and called us to be his peacemakers. Politics is no exception. He's done the hard work at the cross and commissioned us to represent him. When we refuse to love our enemies, however, and don't undertake the hard work of our heavenly Father's business, it harms the family name.

Loving your enemies—political and otherwise—is a fruit of the gospel. It's a way to give what you've received, to be part of your heavenly Father's family business. God calls us as his children to invite the neighbors over for a block-party celebration. To invite even the Hatfields or McCoys, those neighbors you haven't spoken to in years because of some ancient dispute.

Can you imagine a community of former enemies who've now become friends? A "ransomed people for God from every tribe and language and people and nation"?[22] A reconciled kingdom of Palestinians and Israelis, Democrats and Republicans, Russians and Ukrainians, black and white, boomers and millennials? That's a picture of the kingdom of God, made possible through the blood of Christ, feasting together in peace.

Let's work toward becoming that people today.

Reflection Questions

- Do you sense God inviting you to make peace with anyone? Make a list of people with whom you have the opportunity to repair broken relationships or build stronger relationships despite differences.

- Identify one person on your list and prepare for a peacemaking conversation by prayerfully reflecting on the following questions:

  - *What are my motives?*
  - *What do I need to repent of?*
  - *Where might I be misunderstanding?*
  - *What story am I telling myself?*
  - *What are my emotions?*
  - *How can I seek appropriate counsel without gossip or slander?*
  - *What is the specific issue I want to bring up?*
  - *What would it look like to forgive the other person?*
  - *Can I overlook this offense, or will there be ongoing tension I need to resolve?*
  - *What would they need to own for reconciliation to be possible?*

- When it comes to political engagement and discourse, in what areas do you need to remove the log from your own eye?

WHEN TO BE BOLD

We launched Prayer and Action groups at our church during the last election season. These were groups of ten to fifteen people who committed to gathering twice a month for one year around a particular political issue and do the following three things:

1. *Pray together,* seeking King Jesus about their issue.
2. *Learn together,* from curated readings and local leaders working on their issue.
3. *Act together,* finding something concrete they could do locally to make a difference regarding their issue in our city.

Our first two groups were Criminal Justice and Sanctity of Life (the former typically perceived as a left-wing issue, and the latter as a right-wing issue). We wanted people with leanings on both sides of the political aisle to be able to connect in concrete ways on an issue they were passionate about. We pastors were involved in these groups so we could learn alongside people in our congregation. In the years since, new groups formed around other topics, like Affordable Housing, Health and Wellness, At-Risk Youth, and Refugees.

Why *prayer* and *action*? When a national conversation arises, we've regularly seen these pitted against each other. One side says, "God's still on the throne; we're praying!" To which many respond, "Spare us your thoughts and prayers; we need action!" The former can use prayer as an excuse for apathy (and often not actually pray). The latter can grow exhausted and disillusioned while actively involved on their own strength, running on fumes.

We need both prayer *and* action. Through prayer, we have access to the greatest resource at our disposal: the King of the universe! He hears our cries and acts on our behalf, responding to the prayers of his people. This is our secret weapon! We'd be foolish not to use it. Likewise, through action, we want to challenge the tendency, especially in an election season, to be really loud online and really lazy in real life.

There's a temptation to feel valiant while shouting into the dumpster fire that is X (formerly known as Twitter), or arguing in the cesspool of Facebook, while at the mercy of algorithms, with opinions that convince no one and having virtually no real-world impact. While there's a place for online dialogue, what if we were committed to taking concrete action in our neighborhoods? (More on this in chapter 9.) Once we jumped in, many of our Prayer and Action groups found that our city's most pressing challenges on these issues were not what we anticipated.

Further, we discovered concrete ways for us to make a tangible difference.

One big question for you might be, *What issues should we take a stand on?* Does the gospel inform where God's people pray and take action? That's the subject of this chapter: discerning when to speak up and take a stand. While that's not always a simple question with easy answers, a good way to start is by taking a cue from the early church.

FIVE MARKS OF THE EARLY CHURCH

The early church stood out. A renowned historian, the late Larry Hurtado, observed what made Christians distinct in the Roman Empire as a "unique social project," with at least five characteristics that marked their life together:[1]

1. Multiethnic Community
2. Care for the Poor
3. Sexual Ethic
4. Pro-Life with Children
5. Forgiveness and Enemy Love

Let's unpack each. First, *multiethnic community:* Christians ate together with other Christians who were radically different from them. Jew and Gentile, slave and free, male and female. This was radical in the ancient world, where table fellowship was reserved for people who were like you, as a sign of your class and social standing. Yet for the early church, all who gathered around the table were one family, brothers and sisters, united in Christ. They partied together.

These relationships cultivated a category-breaking community; a diverse, reconciled, multiethnic family; a taste of God's kingdom with every nation, tribe, and tongue. It may not seem like a big deal to us, but to ancient eyes, the most shocking thing about the early Christians was their meals: who was coming to dinner.

Second, *care for the poor:* Christians were generous, giving extravagantly of their time, energy, and money. In a world with no social safety net, they provided for the hungry and homeless. In a world with no hospitals, they nursed the sick. In a world where family was everything, they embraced the widow and the orphan. This party welcomed those who couldn't afford much.

Roman emperors were shocked, declaring in disbelief, "The Christians care not only for their own poor but ours as well!"[2]

For the early church, care was the only proper response to the gospel of Christ, who, "though he was rich, . . . for your sake became poor, so that you through his poverty might become rich."[3] God's generosity cultivates a generous people. This had political impact as a major factor in the church's growth as a grassroots movement, spreading like yeast in the dough of society, which would eventually outgrow and outlast the Roman Empire.[4]

Third, *sexual ethic:* The early church held a high bar for sex, marriage, and family. While the Romans were famous for being stingy with their money and generous with their sex, the Christians were famous for being generous with their money and "stingy" with their sex (or, better put, reserving such self-giving for the marriage bed). Sex was reserved for one man and one woman in a lifelong covenant of marriage. This was radically countercultural in Roman society, which was in many ways— particularly for men—even more sexually wild, crazy, and licentious than ours. It was a debaucherous party where powerful men ruled.[5]

Christianity was good for women, who flocked to the church.[6] It benefited children as well, who were raised in more stable, loving families. The early church confronted men's misuse of power in sex and marriage with the call to reflect Christ, who laid down his life for his bride in faithful, covenant love. And in family, with the call to be gentle, not harsh, with their children, reflecting our heavenly Father's patient care, loving discipline, and extravagant embrace of us.[7]

Fourth, *pro-life with children:* The early Christians famously cared for vulnerable children. Infanticide was common in the Roman Empire, where unwanted babies were left out in the cold to die from exposure. Most frequently, these were girls.[8] As one man wrote home to his wife in 1 B.C., "If it is a boy, let it live; if it is a girl, expose it."[9] Abortion was also frequently practiced, often under the pressure of men who didn't want the inconvenience of a child, and with brutal methods that were dangerous for women.

The Christians, in contrast, were well known for scouring the garbage heaps to find discarded infants and bring them into their families as their own. The church confronted abortion, calling out its destruction of life and challenging men to take responsibility for the children they fathered. Christians put their money where their mouth was, spearheading an adoption movement that embodied the heavenly Father's loving embrace.[10] Vulnerable children were welcomed to the party.

Finally, *forgiveness and enemy love:* The early Christians endured backbreaking persecution with unbreakable love. As they were being thrown to the lions, skewered in the arena, and burned at the stake, they offered bold forgiveness to their persecutors as Christ had offered it to them. As they were kicked out of their families and ostracized from polite society, they proactively loved their enemies as Christ had laid down his life for them. They extended the invitation to God's kingdom celebration with their lives. The heart of the gospel was forgiveness, they believed, and they gave as they had received.

The early church was countercultural and strange. They stood out.

Okay, what's that have to do with today? The late pastor Tim Keller made the observation that if you lean Left politically, you probably like numbers 1 and 2 ("multiethnic community" and "care for the poor") but start to squirm a bit when you hear numbers 3 and 4 ("sexual ethic" and "pro-life with children"). If you lean Right politically, the inverse is likely true: You probably get excited about numbers 3 and 4 but start to have questions when people emphasize numbers 1 and 2. And *nobody* likes number 5; "forgiveness and enemy love" are in short supply on both sides of the political aisle these days.[11]

Yet Christian faithfulness boldly holds together all five characteristics.

In our church, we've sought to plant a flag in each of these five areas. We've regularly told our people things like, "Some of you are hoping we'll stop talking about race and justice; others of you are hoping we'll stop talking about sexuality and gender. Yet we're committed to both." We believe both are required for faithfulness to Jesus in our discipleship and witness, even if that means we won't fit into the political boxes of our moment.

I'm not saying these are the only five issues. I love the work of Justin Giboney and the AND Campaign, who model Christlike civic engagement on issues such as immigration, the economy, drug laws, and casinos. They're crossing typical party lines, helping Christians (in the words of their tagline) "to open their Bible and think not like a Democrat, not like a Republican, but like a Christian." Whether or not you agree with them on every issue, they represent a gospel-centered worldview and posture that's working for better political representation, more compassionate policies, and a healthier political culture. Truth Over Tribe is another great organization helping Christians engage beyond partisan lines. You should check them both out.[12]

This is also not saying there's always one clear policy for every political issue. There are underlying questions on things like the ideal role of government, or gray areas for wisdom and discernment on the best public policies that Christians can agree to disagree on. Yet we should approach such questions *as* Christians, with both compassion and conviction, not pretending to be disinterested observers but seeking to love God and our neighbors in the public sphere.

Let's take a closer look at two particular areas: "race and justice" and "sexuality and gender." Why? I've found these to be the most explosive issues in our context and for many churches I know nationally. We'll look at other issues in coming chapters, but these are good case studies on the cost and worthiness of taking a stand.

RACE AND JUSTICE

What was the grenade that blew up the church whose story I opened with in chapter 1? I shared about half her people leaving angrily, but I haven't yet shared the specific catalyst of the mass exodus: the race-and-justice conversation.

It began with Ahmaud Arbery. As the video of his murder at the hands of white vigilantes went viral, one of the pastors posted a message to social media, via video, expressing grief at the event and showing support for black brothers and sisters who were mourning. The response was swift and furious: Why was he "making it about race"?

One phrase he used was jumped upon in particular: "We don't need to wait for the facts." In context, he was clearly saying, *We don't need to wait for the facts in order to grieve this loss of life and join with our brothers and sisters who are hurting.* But this was quickly spun uncharitably, pulled out of the context of his video, and the rumors began flying: *Your church doesn't believe in the justice system. Throw out law and order. Guilty until proven innocent. Facts don't matter, just feelings.*

This is where a handful of influential members left angrily and sought to take down the church. They spread slander and gossip through coffee-shop conversations and email chains, scoured the social media feeds of pastors and their spouses for ammo, and joined a new church that was willing to link arms with their cause and publicly accuse the church of abandoning the gospel.

Our congregation experienced blowback too, as we were relationally connected. Shortly after, I gave a thank-you message to our church. This was in the early days of the pandemic, when our services—like for most churches—went online. Financially, we expected to get hammered, but our people went above and beyond, giving even more. So I thanked them for their generosity, explaining that because of it, the group of congregations we were part of was able to give $1.5 million to churches hardest hit by Covid-19. A large portion of this went to a network of more than twenty (primarily black) churches in the Bronx, New York, and another significant portion to Navajo leaders ministering on reservations in Arizona, both regions massively affected by the pandemic.

This was quickly taken out of context, however, and spread as a rumor that went viral: *Your church is funneling millions of dollars of your tithe money to Black Lives Matter, the organization.* This rumor was simply not true. We had given to gospel-centered, faith-based ministries that we had long-standing relationships with. The New York churches were part of Tim Keller's City to City network. The Navajo leaders were theologically conservative and relatively apolitical. The rumor would have been hilarious if the results weren't so tragic.

A prominent local church started a sermon series against churches like us, raising the alarm on "woke church" and identifying our friend's congregation as culprit number one. (The prominent local church grew exponentially.) Other local leaders said our churches were under the influence of Satan, teaching heresy, and leading God's people astray. It was baseless slander, but many people left because of rumors like these.

Here's the thing: I wouldn't take it back.

I'm not saying we did everything perfectly, but black brothers and sisters in our church—and beyond—regularly said they felt valued, loved, and supported. (Virtually everyone who left was white.) The rest of our church was encouraged to see we didn't back down when the going got tough. Trust was built with multi-ethnic leaders in our city. There's a cost to planting a flag, but if it's planted in gospel soil, the cost is worth it.

Also, it exposed an idol: Those who left their churches were, predominantly, converts to the Religion of Security. After dozens of conversations with those who were willing to talk, security was clearly the primary driver behind the division. Those who left still attended a church, but their primary formation was coming from pundits, partisan media, and the ideological values of their political quadrant. I, for one, would rather have the idol exposed than have it hiding under the carpet.

THE GOSPEL AND RACE

Why was this worth taking a stand on? Because the gospel is all about reconciliation. Jesus died to reconcile us not only to himself but *through* himself to one another. The church is a multi-ethnic community comprised of every nation, tribe, and tongue. Given the complicated, war-torn history of the nations, this means we've got some work to do. Such work, the gospel says, is dear to the heart of God.

We also believe that sin runs deep. Deeper than our actions and behaviors and into the desires of the human heart. Deeper than our stated motives and into the prejudice and resentment that can lurk within. Deeper than our practice as individuals and into the patterns of our surrounding society and culture. Deeper than a leader's season of influence and into the legacy of policies implemented that can impact generations to come.

Yet while sin runs deep, we also believe that grace runs deeper. That Christ is pulling back together what sin has torn apart, to reconcile humanity and restore creation to God.[13] That as Christians, we are to pursue justice, for God himself declares, "I, the LORD, love justice."[14] That in the family of God, we are to "rejoice with those who rejoice; mourn with those who mourn,"[15] sharing life together as brothers and sisters. That biblical justice has implications for our common life together. That as the redeemed, we are to pursue reconciliation, reflecting a Savior who shed his blood to reconcile us to God and one another.[16]

A PLAN OF ACTION

Okay, so what did we do practically to disciple our people in this race-and-justice conversation? We didn't do everything perfectly, and there's no one-size-fits-all approach, but it can be helpful to illustrate what concrete action might look like.

We took a multifaceted approach. For starters, I was part of a small team that wrote an article called "Racism and the Gospel," with input from leadership in our broader network. We sought to give a theological framework for the conversation, explain our convictions, and clarify what we did and did not mean by certain terms. (That resource is available online.)[17] We hosted a livestream event to launch the document, including panels of church leaders and members. Eventually, a shorthand version of the article was included within the convictions of our church membership packet.

Next, we made race and justice part of the broader conversation in our church. We discussed it, when appropriate, in our services. (See chapter 7 for thoughts on how to maturely approach social issues in a church service.) We invited speakers as part of our monthly lecture series. We did podcast interviews with multiethnic leaders from our church community. We created a resource list of recommended books and articles to dive deeper.

We sought to provide clarity. We created an online calendar with fifteen-minute phone-appointment slots, where anyone in our church could easily call a pastor with a question or concern on this or any other area. We did a podcast distinguishing biblical justice from postmodern justice and addressing some of the common questions we'd get about loaded buzzwords like *critical race theory* and *cancel culture*.[18] We started small groups hosted by trusted leaders, centered on our recommended reading, for those who wanted to explore further. We approached the *confused* (who just needed clarity) differently from the *convinced* (who were just looking for a fight; we declined to get in the mud).

We took seriously the concerns of those who were willing to engage, and we got to work. We started a Prayer and Action group on criminal justice, pursuing concrete action to make a positive difference in our city. We directly invited the most vocal people to join in taking action. (Most of them declined.) We partnered with black churches in the Phoenix area, coming behind initiatives they were leading. We supported faith-based organizations like Hustle PHX, equipping underserved entrepreneurs to launch sustainable businesses for the common good.

We stayed at the table together. Long-term change emerges from healthy relationships, so we challenged our people to not let the political tides and cultural currents cause us to drift apart. It's okay to disagree, to have different leanings, to be in process.

But it's not okay to let slander, innuendo, and rumor fracture the body of Christ, tearing apart the unity for which he died. It's not okay to crash Jesus's party.

Planting a flag on race and justice can have a massive impact. A lead pastor at a friend's congregation, wearied from seeing so many friends and people he loved walk away, delivered an ultimatum to his elders: Either leave the network, disown the "Gospel and Race" article, and back away from this conversation, or he would leave. The elders had a heartbreaking decision to make. He was a beloved leader, they were an influential congregation, and their decision would have ripple effects throughout the community.

They were convicted by Paul's words that it is easier for the stronger members of the body to say to the weaker, "I don't need you." In other words, it is easier for those with more power and influence in the church community to dismiss the concerns and perspectives of those with less clout (in this case, a racial minority). Yet the apostle was adamant that such "weaker" members (with less power and influence) are actually indispensable to the health of the body and should be treated with honor.[19]

Although the lead pastor chose to leave, the elders unanimously chose to stay. Through prayer and godly counsel, they believed the church is better together.

They stayed at the table.

I share all this to say that planting a flag can be costly, but it's worth it when planted in gospel territory. In this situation, it was converts to the Religion of Security who were attacking from the Right. But we've also experienced converts to the Religion of Identity attacking from the Left. It's to this second case study that we now turn.

SEXUALITY AND GENDER

We launched a Countercultural Convictions series during the same year the race-and-justice conversation was blowing up. (Talk about being a glutton for punishment!) Our goal was not to be provocative but to equip our people to follow Jesus faithfully in areas that run against the grain of our cultural moment. We addressed a variety of countercultural topics, including two messages on sex and gender. They were compassionate and nuanced but also, well, countercultural.

Our college town leans Left. Tempe is home to Arizona State University, one of the largest college campuses in the country. Roughly 40 percent of our church body is composed of college students and young adults. We also have many professors. Taken together, this means much of our congregation leans Left politically. People were generally stoked when we took a stand on race and justice (unlike our friend's congregation in nearby conservative-leaning Gilbert), but when it came to sexuality and gender, well . . .

An online group targeted our live stream, posting hostile comments to everyone watching. We received angry emails, negative Google reviews warned we were a bigoted hate church, and we had our first protestor in this season. Fun times.

It wasn't just outsiders. A few leaders and longtime members in our church stepped down in this season, explicitly citing the Christian sexual ethic amid the LGBTQ+ conversation. Some had been deconstructing for a while over a variety of issues and had been fine knowing what we believed as long as we were quiet about it, but articulating our beliefs on a Sunday caused discomfort.

The cultural pressure is real. Over the years, there have been times as a pastor where I've fielded a question a week about

Christian teaching on sexuality. It can be easy to wrestle with whether or not the topic is really a big deal. Should we ignore it and avoid what could be a stumbling block?

While costly, faithfulness in this arena is worth it. We've seen marriages restored, people who've experienced the pain of divorce find healing in Christ, and men and women with porn addiction come out of the darkness of shame and into the light of grace. We've seen singles find encouragement to be all Christ made them to be without needing to be married. We've seen boyfriends and girlfriends seek to reflect the sanctity of Christ's love to each other in their sexual faithfulness before God. We've seen people attracted to the same sex find their struggles compassionately included in our shared life as a church family with intimacy and union in Christ. We've seen the bride of Christ built up to experience the glory of faithfulness with Christ our Groom and anticipate the party that's coming in the wedding feast at the end of the world.[20]

THE GOSPEL AND SEX

Why was this worth being bold on? God's vision for sex is beautiful, more beautiful and compelling than anything our culture has to offer. I believe that sex, marriage, family, and singleness are designed to point to greater things, like the intimacy and faithfulness we were designed for in union with Christ; like the life-giving power of the Spirit, who makes us children of God; like the eternal communion-of-love who is the triune God. (My book *Beautiful Union* focuses on these themes and came out of this season of ministry.)[21]

Marital love is designed to point to the love of God.

I also believe we're all in the same boat. That this is *much* bigger than the LGBTQ+ conversation (even if our culture puts that front and center), as God's vision is countercultural when it comes to divorce, adultery, premarital sex, pornography, abortion, and more. We believe that the gospel frees us from guilt and shame because we're all sexually broken sinners at the foot of the cross, invited to come to the only One whose sexuality is not broken, Jesus, and receive the mercy we all need that he's all too happy to give.

I believe in a high vision of singleness—that Jesus was single and Paul was single, so if you're single, you're in good company. That the New Testament and historic church have esteemed singleness as a vocation equal, if not preferable, to marriage and we're invited to join them. That you can have the reality without the sign, the movie without the sneak preview, the union with Christ you were made for without marriage that points to it. You can skip the appetizer and enjoy the meal. Whether married or single, you can experience union with God.

A PLAN OF ACTION

So, what did we do? Again, there's no magic blueprint, but here are a few things we tried. In conjunction with the Countercultural Convictions series, I was part of a small team that wrote articles on both sex and gender for our church to clarify our theological convictions and give guidance. These were eventually incorporated into our membership packet.

We hosted a Sexual Wholeness Conference with Jay Stringer (he's amazing—check him out) that explored how sexual brokenness can reveal our way to healing. For those struggling with porn addiction, we started care groups rooted in a grace-filled (rather than shame-based) approach. We revamped our premarital and marital counseling process to integrate top-notch resources and best serve couples in our church. We cast a high vision for singleness as a vocation equal to marriage in the kingdom.

We held a church-wide event on gender to equip our people on this pressing cultural conversation. We listened to the voices of those who experience gender dysphoria. We transformed our men's and women's ministries to steer away from gender stereotypes while creating meaningful opportunities for connection and relationship. I led a gender forum, with about eighty people over multiple weeks around tables, where we dove deeper into the relevant theological and practical issues. We hosted a gathering for parents in order to equip them with a healthy way to talk to their kids about sex and gender.

In addition to sermons, we used our monthly TED Talk–style lecture event and our podcast to bring in first-class speakers and interview relevant people within our congregation. We equipped small-group leaders to host meaningful conversations in their gatherings. We created a recommended-resources list for people wanting to explore further.

* * *

Again, I am not saying we did everything perfectly. But I am saying that seeking to be equipped in these areas was worth investing time, energy, and intentionality. You don't have to do things the same way, but you can start small and feel the freedom to set a course and pace that makes sense for your context.

Being bold is about more than posting a statement on social media; it's about equipping disciples to live faithfully to Jesus. It's about more accurately reflecting our King and his better party to the world.

KEEP CHRISTIANITY WEIRD

We have a slogan in my hometown: Keep Portland Weird. It's plastered in black and yellow on bumper stickers, signs, and murals across the city. And for good reason. We're a top destination for the most tattooed and vegan hipsters and hippies. A bikeable beer town that is environmentally green, pot friendly, dog friendly—and doesn't fluoridate its water.

We celebrate the eccentric, curious, and strange, as lampooned in the hit show *Portlandia*. You can find unicycling Darth Vaders playing bagpipes with fire, enjoy watching dozens of glamorous homemade go-karts racing down an extinct volcano in the Adult Soapbox Derby, or find yourself (as I once accidentally did) surrounded by ten thousand naked bike riders at the world's largest annual World Naked Bike Ride.

We don't run from the weirdness; we embrace it (though, to be clear, I'm not endorsing naked bike rides).

Jesus wants us to embrace the weirdness. Not the weirdness of Portland per se, but the weirdness of his kingdom. When you embrace the King, you don't fit into the typical boxes of Republican or Democrat, Left or Right. You'll have a hard time fully making your home in any of the four political religions. You'll stand out; people will look at you with suspicion. You'll become a party crasher, like Jesus, who refuses to conform to the partisan boxes, boundaries, and scripts.

Yet Jesus is calling you to celebrate his eccentricity, to embrace the weirdness.[22] There's a scene I love where Jesus told his followers, "Eat my flesh; drink my blood."[23] The crowds freaked out (*Yikes! Cannibalism!*) and ran for the hills. He was talking about the Lord's Supper (which we'll talk about in chapter 7), but the disciples understandably took offense: "This is a hard saying; who can listen to it?"[24] In other words, *Jesus, you made it weird!*

Jesus responded, "What if you were to see the Son of Man ascending to where he was before?"[25] He's telling them, *You'll see even stranger things.* Jesus was talking about his ascension to the right hand of God's royal throne, where he'll be exalted as King of the world. But that's an odd image: a Galilean carpenter levitating in the skies. So more followers freaked out: "After this many of his disciples turned back and no longer walked with him."[26] They took off, thinking, *This guy's crazy!*

Yet Jesus was undisturbed. Jesus was saying to embrace the strange. Don't try to normalize his kingdom; wrap your arms around it. It's an upside-down kingdom, where the last become first, the greatest are those willing to become the least, the call to truly live is to come and die, and the foolishness of God triumphs over the wisdom of the world.[27] He's a strange King: born in a manger, feasting with tax collectors and prostitutes, sneaking away from the applauding masses, and choosing the cross as his location for coronation as King.[28]

Like Kyle's high school parties (mentioned in the introduction), the strangeness is part of the beauty. Too many of us try to accommodate Jesus to our political parties, to our cultural ideologies, to make him more palatable to our social circles and personal preferences. But Jesus isn't having it. Don't try to fit him into your box; let him pull you out of yours. Out of the claustrophobic boxes of the four political religions and into the expansive kingdom of God, where Jesus's slogan is plastered all around town.

KEEP CHRISTIANITY WEIRD.

STRANGE BUT TRUE

Christianity is strange but true. Jesus asked the twelve if they were going to leave him too. Peter gave the classic response: "Lord, to whom shall we go? You have the words of eternal life."[29] Basically, *You're weird, Jesus, but you're true. Your strange kingdom is where life is found.*

Christianity's strangeness is the source of its power. For example, if you were to interview people on the street, asking, "What is the biggest problem the world faces today?" some might mention political corruption, sex trafficking, or global poverty. A Christian, however, might faithfully answer, "Our world's biggest problem is that two naked vegetarians listened to a talking snake in a garden and ate a forbidden pomegranate."[30]

That answer is strange but true. It says there is a deeper root behind the problems in our world. That we were made for intimacy and union with God but that our attempt to rule the earth on our own, our desire to be *like* God rather than *with* God, has led to our distance and alienation *from* God. Our grasp for power from the True King has *poisoned* us and our world!

Similarly, if you were to ask, "What's the greatest hope for the world today?" some might say that it's political reform, a new stimulus package, or better education. A Christian, however, might faithfully answer, "Our greatest hope is that a first-century executed Galilean carpenter is coming back on a flying white horse with a tattoo on his thigh and a sword sticking out of his mouth to set it all straight."[31]

That answer is strange, but the strangeness is the source of its power. It says that we need help from beyond ourselves, that we can't fix this world on our own, and that the One who willingly gave his life in obscurity is the One whom God has entrusted to set all things right. The Lamb who was humble enough to work through weakness is also the Lion who is powerful enough to put evil in its place and restore creation. Oh yeah, and guess what that tattoo on his thigh says?

KING OF KINGS AND LORD OF LORDS[32]

We follow a strange King who rules a strange kingdom. Let's be like the early church and break the boxes the empire expects us to stay confined within. Let's throw a better party, where we stop trying to domesticate Jesus and instead let our curiosity drive us to him, discovering that his eccentricity is where life is found. Let's stop trying to run from the hard sayings at which many take offense and instead plant a flag with the King in the soil of his upside-down kingdom, even if it makes us look crazy in the eyes of the world.

It's a strange kingdom, indeed. For it deals with not only *what* you stand for but *how* you stand when you stand with a strange King.

Reflection Questions

- If you had the opportunity to launch a Prayer and Action group about a particular issue, what would the issue be? Who would you want to join you?

- We discussed five marks of the early church. Which of these five is easiest for you to embrace? Which is most challenging?

  1. Multiethnic Community
  2. Care for the Poor
  3. Sexual Ethic
  4. Pro-Life with Children
  5. Forgiveness and Enemy Love

- If you boldly embraced all five of these characteristics, what would the cost be? How would it impact your life? Spend some time asking God to give you courage to be bold in areas that are uncomfortable for you.

AN OUTPOST OF THE KINGDOM

"Are we going to say anything?" As a church leadership team, we regularly find ourselves asking this question. *Say anything about what?* you might be asking. Take your pick: the latest mass shooting, political controversy, national church scandal, or international crisis. We increasingly find ourselves, in our social media age, discerning whether to speak to a particular event in an upcoming Sunday service. And if so, how to do it well.

There's a tension. On the one hand, we need to shepherd people through the real-life tragedies, confusing turbulence, and emotionally weighted drama that is our modern world. On the other hand, there's a danger of pastors becoming pundits, one more voice crowding the cluttered airwaves with hot takes. (News flash: Mine often aren't that good!) You shouldn't expect your pastor to be an expert on all things. (And, pastors, you don't need to try to be.) Churches can simply become one more platform for the latest political drama.

This reduction of Christianity's calling stifles spiritual growth.

We all face this tension (not just church leaders); I know you feel it. You often wonder, *Do I need to have an opinion on this crisis or that news story? Should I post about it? Should I bring it up in my small group? Should I talk to my kids about it? If my pastor brings it up in the sermon, how will I respond?*

America has a new national liturgy: "the crisis of the week." This regular rhythm shapes and forms us, with habits that have an impact on the people we're becoming. You don't have to go looking for the latest unfolding drama; it bulldozes right into your brain. You enter your phone like a cathedral, where news cycles craft clickbait titles like stained-glass windows into the broader world, and social media feeds clamor for your attention like a call to worship. You find yourself surrounded by a chorus of voices that spike your endorphins, offer belonging, provoke your rage, incite anxiety, and demand—if you are to prove yourself faithful—a response.

Am I going to say anything? If so, what am I going to say?

We all feel this pressure.

How do we remain healthy in this environment? How can we not only stay sane but also thrive in a partisan culture? How do we stay true to the better party Jesus is throwing? I want to offer you formational practices for a polarized world. In this chapter, we'll start with "gathered" practices (things we do gathered as the church together). Then, in the next chapter, we'll move to "scattered" practices (things we can do scattered in our everyday lives beyond Sunday).

Some of these practices may seem mundane, but I want to show you how even such taken-for-granted rhythms can have powerful political significance to form us as the party of our King.

GATHERED PRACTICES

Let's walk through one of our church's typical Sunday services. Not because we're all that creative or unique (these are common historic practices), but because I want to show you how inherently political these church practices are. They are designed to form us into a particular type of people.

Liturgy is a fancy word that basically means rhythms and rituals—things we regularly do. (You probably have a daily liturgy of making your bed and brushing your teeth.)[1] The insight of liturgy is that these habits can become second nature over time. Do something enough and that practice can shape and form you into a particular kind of person.

Church liturgy is designed to do that, but it helps to know what the elements mean. A typical Sunday service is brimming with political significance.

Call to Worship

Our services start with a call to worship. This is the "Behold your God!" moment, orienting our attention to who God is and what he's done. Ideally, the call is not "Hey, everybody, let's worship!" (with an emphasis on our action); it is a pulling back of the curtain to unveil, "Here's the One we've come to worship!" (with an emphasis on who God is, as the object of our adoration).

Who is this God? He is our heavenly Father, who forms us as his family. He is our resurrected Savior, who rescues us from the grave. He is the life-giving Spirit, who renews our affections from the inside out. He is Provider, Redeemer, Sustainer, and Healer. The Lion and Lamb. The Shepherd and Judge. The Bread of Life and the Living Water. The Great I Am, who was, and is, and is to come. I could go on, but one more for our purposes here: the King, who forms us as citizens of his kingdom.

What does this have to do with politics? Everything. We start with God. That's what this aspect of the liturgy is designed to train and cultivate in us. Our starting point is not *what we do* but rather *who God is*. The book of Revelation confronts the Roman Empire by pointing to the nonstop worship service happening right now—above Caesar's head—around God's heavenly throne. There's a higher throne, a greater King, a bigger kingdom.

So stop trying to fit God into the smallness of your party, and instead orient your life around the bigness of his. Don't make God a pawn in your preconceived agenda, political or otherwise; renew your pledge of allegiance to him as King. We dethrone the idols of the political religions when we orient our lives around God's eternal throne. Let go of the pressure of feeling that the world rests on your shoulders (you weren't made to bear that weight!); recognize that it rests on his.

Let the rhythm of worship call your heart to the reminder it needs to hear: The world revolves around him.

Confession and Lament

After the call to worship and a song typically oriented around the bigness of God, we move into a time of confession. Here we turn from the external to the internal, from an awareness of God to an awareness of ourselves before God. We bring before him our shortcomings and failures, knowing he is our heavenly Father waiting with arms outstretched to receive us. We bring him our sins of commission (things we've done) and sins of omission (things we've left undone), knowing he is our Savior who has already done the work and there is nothing left to do but receive.

Lament is also appropriate in this space. We can lament not only the brokenness in our lives but the brokenness in our world. We've frequently utilized this space in our Sunday service when national tragedy has hit: to grieve the loss of life in a mass shooting, to mourn the failed witness of another church scandal, to process the disillusionment around one more political controversy, to cry for help when another natural disaster or war leaves a wake of devastation.

We take it to God.

These are typically corporate prayers, written in advance. We aim for these to be more *priestly* than *pundit*—less giving our opinions to the masses in a veiled diatribe, more bringing our collective pain in a Godward direction, together through prayer. Yet we also aim to be *specific*—not "We grieve the bad events in the news this week," but "We grieve the nineteen children and two teachers killed by a gunman at Uvalde this week. We lament the violence, loss of life, and broader pattern of mass shootings that have become all too common in our society."

What's this have to do with politics? Everything. We don't need to ignore the problems in our world. We don't need to shut down our hearts, to just become emotionless beings who think God only cares about "spiritual things." It's a mistake to assume God is unconcerned with the brokenness—political or otherwise—that is very real and crashing in all around us. We can bring it all before God.

More so, we don't need to ignore the problems in our own lives. The brokenness is not just "out there" but "in here." As the Russian dissident Aleksandr Solzhenitsyn famously puts it, "The line separating good and evil passes not through states, nor between classes, nor between political parties either—but right through every human heart."[2] This part of the liturgy trains us to look within ourselves, to recognize the evil that exists inside us—that we have participated in—and to bring our disease before the Great Physician, who loves to heal.

Confession breeds humility. In a polarized world, it's designed to make you the kind of person who takes the plank out of your own eye before removing the speck from your neighbor's. It trains you to trade your microscope for a mirror, examining your own faults rather than highlighting the flaws of your opponent. I, for one, think that's desperately needed in our political climate today.

Confession is a rhythm of grace. It reminds us of our need for God's mercy—and his extravagant willingness to extend it. Those who've been forgiven much, Jesus tells us, love much.[3] When you experience God's radical forgiveness, when you recognize your desperate need for grace, it trains you to extend forgiveness and grace to others and welcome them to the party.

Again, "Whoever has been forgiven little," Jesus says, "loves little."[4] I wonder if a primary problem in our partisan culture—a major reason we love so little—is we've lost sight of God's forgiveness. We haven't embraced the gospel, in which we're embraced by God, or we've forgotten how sweet and undeserved that embrace is. That's why we're all so angry, all trying to push ourselves up by pressing our opponents down, all trying to prove ourselves to the world. We can break free from that culture, however, when we recognize how desperately in need of grace we are and how relentlessly ready God is to extravagantly give it.

That's what confession is designed to do.

Scripture and Sermon

The reading of Scripture and its exposition in a sermon also play central roles in our service. This is the power of God's Word spoken redemptively into our broken condition. We are children gathered around our heavenly Father, together in his living room, seeking to hear his voice and desire for our lives. We are citizens gathered around Christ our King, listening for his direction for us as his people.

This liturgical pattern shapes our lives around God's story.[5] There are a lot of competing stories in our world: the story of consumerism (You'll find fulfillment when you acquire enough stuff); the story of hedonism (Life is short—do whatever makes you feel good); the story of power (Might makes right, so do whatever you can to get ahead). These stories ultimately can't fulfill us, because they're ultimately not true.

God's Word re-narrates our world. Gathering around the public reading of Scripture is a political act, offering a counter-formation to the false stories of the empire by shaping a community around the true story of the world. For the gospel sets us free as citizens of the kingdom aligning our lives around the story of the King.

Let the King speak to you through his Word. Allow the Spirit to bring fresh truth to your heart, mind, and circumstances. Ideally, a sermon should expose your idols, comfort your wounds, convict you of your failures, cover you in grace, and call you to faithfulness, making clear the implications of the gospel for your life.

There's a place for reading Scripture personally, too (which we'll discuss in the next chapter), but there's also something powerful in the public reading of Scripture, gathering as a community around the biblical story and seeking to be shaped by the Author, who is the true center of the world. Listen not just to hear what you want to hear but to allow God's Word to re-narrate your world.

Communion and Worship

Finally, we celebrate communion—or the Lord's Supper—in a context of worship. The bread and wine are signs of Christ's body given and blood shed to make us his people. This is the climax of our liturgy as we come to the King's table, where we lay down our idols and he gives us himself to form us as citizens of his kingdom.

We come to Jesus for life. That's what this rhythm should form in us. Christ is truly present in the bread and wine. There's mystery here. Different traditions disagree on *how* exactly Christ is present in the elements, but virtually every tradition agrees— whether Reformed, Lutheran, Catholic, Anglican, Orthodox— that Christ is, somehow, truly and mysteriously, through the power of his Spirit, present. The King invites us to his table not just to give us a meal but to give us himself.

Real presence.

Okay, so what does this have to do with politics? Everything. The hope of the world is the presence of Jesus. The greatest thing we have to offer the world—more than our strategies, opinions, and policies, as important as those may be—is the presence of Jesus. This table is at the center of his party, as a foretaste of the kingdom, where we're united with the presence of our King.

At our church, we end every sermon with an invitation to Jesus. "As we come to the table . . ." is our catchphrase, where we connect the theme of that morning to who Jesus is. If it was a message on David and Goliath, we're invited to Jesus the Courageous One, who overcame our giant of sin and death, through his body and blood, so we no longer need to cower in fear. If it was a message on the good Samaritan, we're invited to Jesus the Compassionate One, who saw us beaten and bloody on the side of the road and paid the cost—through his body and blood—to rescue and restore us.[6]

Sometimes people ask, "Why don't we do an altar call at the end of every service?" (What they mean is an evangelistic gospel presentation some churches do every week for people who don't know Jesus.) My response is, "We *do* have an altar call every week!" Only it's for *all* of us. If you're a follower of Jesus, you're invited to come to the table, a sign of the true altar where he sacrificed himself to reconcile you to God. If you're not a follower of Jesus, you're invited to become one so you can share in his life. But for all of us who are citizens of the kingdom, we're invited to come to the King's table and lay down our idols—political and otherwise—to share in the life of the King.

We come to the table in a context of worship. We sing the bulk of our songs here in our liturgy, at the end of the service during communion. Singing is our pledging allegiance, a response of worship to who God is and what he's done.

Worship is not something we do to try to "bring God down"; it is our celebration of the God who has lifted us up—through the life, death, and resurrection of Christ. The King is at the right hand of God's heavenly throne, giving himself to us through his Spirit here on earth. We celebrate around his table and feast as the King shares his life with us and forms us for his kingdom today.

What's more worthy of worship than that?

Baptism

Baptism is a political act. Its imagery is rooted in the Exodus story.[7] As God parted the Red Sea to rescue his people from Egypt, so he parts the waters of baptism to deliver us from the powers of the world. God calls the church out of the old order of things and into life with him in his kingdom.

Baptism is a pledge of allegiance to the King of kings. It's a sign of your political identity. Christian, you serve Christ. When you came up out of the waters, you were sealed as a citizen of his kingdom and given a passport with your new identity.

Your ultimate allegiance is no longer to the contemporary Egypts and Romes of the world—whether America, China, or Nigeria—who seek to rule the earth on their own. You have "dual citizenship," still participating in the civic life of this passing age (we're not in the promised land yet), but also being an outpost of Christ's kingdom, an embassy of his life-giving reign, a foretaste amid the rebellious powers of the world of the age to come.

Live into your identity.

Baptism is a sign of our political character. We are to be a people who die unto self (like going down under the waters) to live unto God (trusting him to raise us up). This means your highest goal in the political arena is not success but faithfulness. You can let go of the old world's ways that grasp for power and cling to control, to be grasped by the ways of God's new creation, which pulls us up into a kingdom of life and love.

"Remember your baptism!" the old adage goes. When you're tempted by our partisan culture, remember your baptism. It shows us the shape of the Christian life: dying and rising with Jesus. It's a "J-curve," to borrow a phrase from author Paul Miller, that goes down (like the front curve of the *J*) in order to be raised up even higher (like the back curve of the *J*).[8] We are a people who vulnerably surrender our lives into God's hands when faithfulness requires, trusting him to lift us up from the chaotic waters that surround us and exalt us to an even higher place, seated with Christ.

You can trust him.

Baptism is not a push-up, where you use your own strength to descend into the waters, then flex your muscles to push yourself back out. No, it's a flat-on-your-back dependence. You need God to grab hold of you by the mighty strength of *his* arms and lift you up out of the grave. Baptism is a sign of grace. You're a person who relies on God's strength—however crazy the world around you might get, you're safe and secure in him. You can give grace, as one who's received grace. You can forgive, as you've been forgiven. It didn't start with your effort; it won't end with it either.

Baptism reminds you who you are and whose you are.

You belong to Christ the King.

We are a new-exodus people. We've been delivered through the waters from our enslavement to sin, Satan, and death. We are on our way to the promised land of God's eternal kingdom. In the meantime, we sojourn through the wilderness of this world, like Israel of old, dependent on God's provision in the desert. We are an in-between people. Our home is not in Egypt behind us, nor with the giants in Canaan before us, nor with the hostile nations who surround us.

Our home is with God.

Jesus feeds us in the wilderness. His body is the greater bread, like manna in the desert, that sustains us on the journey.[9] His blood the greater sacrifice, like the Passover Lamb of old, that marks us as his people.[10] His words the greater instruction, for we do not live on bread alone but on the eternal Word, which proceeds from the mouth of God.[11] His Spirit the greater cloud by day and fire by night to guide us on the journey, until we arrive at our destination in the promised land with God.[12] Jesus leads us in the wilderness by giving us himself.

Baptism and Eucharist are political acts. These sacraments, foundational to the identity of God's people, are designed to shape our self-understanding and to form us as a distinct political community, marking the church as an outpost of the kingdom of God.[13]

We are citizens of his kingdom.

*   *   *

Jesus is throwing a better party. These practices are meant to help you join it. One of the most powerful political practices you undertake might be attending church—shockingly, perhaps, even more powerful than what you post on social media—if you allow its rhythms to form you the way they're designed to, that is. Gathering around God's Word and sacrament, with God's people, in a context of worship can help you thrive in a partisan culture and stay sane in a polarized world.

We've talked about *gathered* practices; let's now turn to *scattered* practices. In the next chapter, we'll explore how formational practices in our personal lives can make us better political disciples of the King.

Reflection Questions

- Think back to the last sermon you heard and reflect on any possible implications for your conduct in the political realm (even if the sermon was not explicitly on anything political).

- Using Psalm 13 as a template, write a prayer of lament, where you bring anything sad, broken, or unjust in our world that captures your heart into the presence of God. Be attentive to the local, national, and global issues that grieve you most.

- Which of these gathered practices stood out to you as one that you possibly want to be more attentive to?

  1. Call to Worship
  2. Confession and Lament
  3. Scripture and Sermon
  4. Communion and Worship
  5. Baptism

FORMATIONAL PRACTICES
FOR A POLARIZED WORLD

"You woke idiots don't care about our country!" Sebastian lost it. He exploded on his small group and went on a ten-minute volatile tirade before storming out of the house and slamming the front door. Sebastian knew these people well; he'd been part of this church small group that met weekly for a while. But what had started as a fairly benign conversation quickly went south.

That week, the group was processing God's heart for justice. Sebastian, a recent convert to the Religion of Security, considered all such talk to be propaganda for the Left. So when someone made a comment he didn't like, he lost it and blasted the group as a whole.

Sebastian met with one of our pastors later that week to explain why he was leaving the church. Rather than engage in a back-and-forth on specific cultural issues, our pastor asked him if he'd be willing to prayerfully read through the book of James together over the coming weeks. Sebastian had never read the book of James before. In fact, he confessed that his intake of Scripture came mostly from a diet of podcasts, with bits and pieces of singular verses pulled out rather than him studying whole books of the Bible.

Over the coming months, they studied the book of James

together. Their goal was to seek a view of public engagement shaped by God's Word rather than media talking points. Sebastian was transformed. He came back to his community group and repented, apologizing for his blowup and admitting that the influence of certain news outlets had shaped his view more than God's Word.

He still leaned into the Security quadrant but said he was gripped by God's vision for "the power of the tongue" in the book of James, with a high calling for how we use our words, and for "true religion" that cares for widows, orphans, and the oppressed. Jesus crashed his party and called him to a better one, where he could bring his lean but needed to submit his bow. Sebastian discovered that reading Scripture is more than a "spiritual" activity.

It's a formational practice for a polarized world.

* * *

In the previous chapter, we explored how our gathered practices as the church are meant to form us as political disciples of the kingdom. Our formation is not only in such gathered practices, however, but also our scattered practices. Let's move beyond the Sunday worship service to our everyday lives as God's people. Here we want to reimagine how common Christian practices—like prayer, shared meals, and fasting—can shape our political formation.[1] Let's start with the practice Sebastian found so powerful: reading Scripture.

READING SCRIPTURE

What do true-crime dramas, Joe Rogan interviews, and MrBeast stunts have in common? They're staples in America's information diet. Even when the content is not explicitly political, it's shaping us as citizens. Now, I love podcasts and enjoy social media, but I've noticed a trend: For many Christians, this flood of information pushes out any time for engaging God's Word.

This nutrient deficiency in our information diet forms citizens who are full of facts and anecdotes but whose hearts are hungry for something more substantive. As Brett McCracken observes in *The Wisdom Pyramid*, living off podcasts, social media, and clickbait articles is like subsisting on junk food.[2] It's a tasty treat but a bad foundation for a healthy diet. We need nutrient-rich fare, too—like Scripture, Christian community, nature, books, and creativity.

Let's re-prioritize reading Scripture. There is nourishment in God's Word. The King of kings speaks through his Word to form us as an alternative people amid the kingdoms of this world. Immersing ourselves in the biblical story helps us discern and resist the false and idolatrous stories narrated to us by the principalities and powers behind the political quadrants.

We need the whole Bible. There's a temptation to focus only on the bits we like. Here are some examples:

- *The Progress quadrant* tends to elevate the call of Genesis 1–2 to be culture makers who shape the world while downplaying the power of sin and devastation of the Fall.

- *The Responsibility quadrant* tends to prefer the practical wisdom of Proverbs and straightforward instruction of Paul's epistles while downplaying the prophets and stories of the Old Testament that denounce systemic injustice and corruption.

- *The Identity quadrant* tends to love the bold call to justice found in the prophets and the dignity of the image of God while shying away from the Gospels' call to deny yourself, take up your cross, and obey God over your desires.

- *The Security quadrant* tends to be drawn to passages about spiritual warfare and apocalyptic books like Revelation while downplaying the call to love those unlike you in the good-Samaritan and "one another" accounts of the New Testament, or concern for the immigrant sojourner throughout the Old Testament.

That's like eating only broccoli. You will get important nutrients, but the lack of calories will deplete your energy. If you eat enough broccoli to meet your daily caloric requirement, you'll find yourself with unspeakable gastrointestinal issues.

Similarly, some of us have an imbalanced diet of Scripture, and it depletes our souls. We miss out on the richer tastes and important nutrients found in other biblical "food groups." Our minds don't think clearly about important issues, we find ourselves sluggish in obedience, and we release verbal flatulence into the world.

Most of us don't do this deliberately but rather find ourselves subconsciously drawn to the same books and same passages time and time again. A good Bible-reading plan can help you engage the whole biblical story.

Regular Scripture reading will also help you guard against misuse of the Bible. Historically, people twisted Scripture to justify the slave trade or Holocaust. Today, the four political quadrants can do this in more subtle ways.

- *The Religion of Progress:* Regarding sending troops to Afghanistan, President Biden said, "Those who have served through the ages have drawn inspiration from the Book of Isaiah, when the Lord says, 'Whom shall I send . . . who shall go for us?' And the American military has been answering for a long time: 'Here am I, Lord. Send me. Here I am. Send me.'"[3] Yet this Isaiah passage is not about a military superpower sending troops to protect national interests; it's about a prophet being sent to confront corruption among the people of God.

- *The Religion of Responsibility:* Many have used Jesus's statement "The poor you will always have with you"[4] to justify an apathy toward seeking to alleviate poverty. Yet Jesus was alluding to Deuteronomy 15:11, which is a call to generosity, where the persistence of poverty among God's people is a sign of their unfaithfulness and rebellion, their failing to care for the poor and vulnerable as God has called them to. In context, Jesus's statement is *indicting,* not *justifying,* God's people.[5]

- *The Religion of Identity:* Many have used Jesus's famous statement "Do not judge, or you too will be judged"[6] as a call to live and let live, to justify a "You do you" mentality that would never question someone else's choices or lifestyle. Although Jesus does confront a judgmental posture toward others, his emphasis in the surrounding passage is on pursuing holiness in our own lives before God so that we can help one another as his community of disciples. We cannot get away from the call in the New Testament to exercise discernment and judgment with one another.[7] Jesus is raising the bar on the call to obedience, not lowering it.

- *The Security Quadrant:* When Donald Trump was asked what his favorite verse in the Bible was, he responded, "An eye for an eye," explaining, "That's not a particularly nice thing. But . . . when you see what's going on with our country, how people are taking advantage of us, and how they scoff at us and laugh at us. . . . They laugh at our face, and they're taking our jobs, they're taking our money, they're taking the health of our country. . . . We have to be firm and have to be very strong. And we can learn a lot from the Bible, that I can tell you."[8] Actually, Jesus explicitly calls his followers to a higher bar—one of nonretaliation.[9] There's a place for governmental justice and national security, but Jesus warns against a fear-based "Us versus Them" mentality.

This twisting of verses is like processed food, which has been significantly transformed from its natural state. Bell peppers, tomatoes, corn, onions, and garlic can all form a nourishing salad—but are also all found in a bag of Doritos. Such ingredients are healthy when eaten as whole food but when highly processed can become substantially less nutritious or even harmful to our bodies.

Similarly, Bible verses can be "highly processed" through the political ideologies. This happens when we extract them (like ingredients) out of context or inject them (like additives) with unbiblical ideas. You may modify and manipulate them to become highly palatable, but they also become significantly less healthful.

I'm not saying you should never quote Bible verses. (I've been quoting many in this book!) I'm saying we must understand them within the whole biblical story. Don't assume the Bible affirms your political ideology.

In *The Drama of Scripture,* theologian Michael Goheen argues that there's a great danger when we break the Bible into little bits that warm our hearts, because we can pluck these bits out of the broader sweep of the biblical story and into an idolatrous cultural story:

Many of us have read the Bible as if it were merely a mosaic of little bits—theological bits, moral bits, historical-critical bits, sermon bits, devotional bits. But when we read the Bible in such a fragmented way, we ignore its divine author's intention to shape our lives through its story. . . . Hence the unity of Scripture is no minor matter: a fragmented Bible may actually produce theologically orthodox, morally upright, warmly pious idol worshipers![10]

Catch that last sentence: There's a way to read the Bible that may actually produce "theologically orthodox, morally upright, warmly pious idol worshipers!" Translation: We may ascribe to true bullet points of doctrine but be living out of a false story in our culture.

Each of the four political religions is rooted in a story. Beware inserting Bible verses into the Story of Progress: *We can fix the world's problems with enough technology, education, and innovation.* Or the Story of Responsibility: *Life is all about working hard, so take care of yourself and those depending on you.* Or the Story of Identity: *You do you! Look within and express that to the world.* Or the Story of Security: *We need to defend ourselves from the outsiders threatening our way of life.* While there's an element of truth to each of these stories (see chapter 1), again, they ultimately can't fulfill us—because they're not *ultimately* true.

Here's a prescription: Find a good Bible-reading plan that takes you through the whole biblical story. (I recommend Bible-Project's reading plans, with their accompanying videos and resources to help you understand the context of what you are reading.)[11] This will help you identify when you're being offered theological Doritos by our culture (God offers better food at his party!) and empower you to live counterculturally by immersing yourself in the story of the world's true King.

Your information diet will determine what occupies your mind all day, shapes your conversations, and narrates the story you're living in. Just as our physical lives are sustained by what we take into our bodies, our hearts and minds are nourished by the Word of God.

TABLE FELLOWSHIP

Want to know one of the best ways to avoid converting to a political religion? Hang out with believers who lean in different directions. As we saw in chapter 6, that was a major way the early church transformed the ancient world. Though it may seem simple, the following is part of our "political strategy" as a church: We have small groups that meet in homes around a table. (Groundbreaking, I know.) Here's the countercultural part: We seek to gather beyond affinity, we get to know one another's stories, and we stay at the table together.

This is more difficult than it sounds. In what many have called "The Big Sort," Americans have increasingly sorted themselves into communities of "sameness."[12] We've relocated to neighborhoods where most people share our similar interests and beliefs. Online, this trend is intensified, as our social networks and information sources become echo chambers where everyone thinks the same (and attacks those who don't). Our bubbles can quickly become like high school cliques.

Sadly, many today also choose churches based on political or lifestyle leanings. I've seen this in our city—and in our own church. Some people have left our church over perceived political differences, as I've shared in earlier chapters. Others visit our church thinking they've found their tribe, only to be disappointed when butting up against people who don't share their political vision.

This is dangerous. Studies have shown that when people group together with similar leanings, they drift toward the most extreme perspectives. As Bill Bishop, author of *The Big Sort*, puts it, "Mixed company moderates; like-minded company polarizes. Heterogeneous communities restrain group excesses; homogeneous communities march toward the extremes."[13] In other words, a community without a diversity of leanings will march toward the destructiveness of idolatry.

Beware the march.

Rooting out such differences hinders our mission of loving and reaching our neighbors. This trend toward division looks bleak for the future but is also an incredible opportunity. We can create a common table in a conflicted world. If we can resist the temptation to turn our churches into affinity groups with Jesus tacked on, we can help one another resist the idolatry in our respective camps and see the goodness in different political leanings. We can experience countercultural relationships centered on Jesus as King.

This boosts discipleship. Those who lean toward the Progress quadrant can show us how to create and cultivate for the good of our neighbors. Those who lean toward the Responsibility quadrant can show us how to care for our families and steward the gifts God has given us. Those who lean Identity can remind us of the God of justice, who calls us to care for the oppressed. Those who lean Security can help us see there are evil forces in the world that need to be resisted.

Such a community would be prophetic in a society where we increasingly have meaningful relationships with only those who share our perspectives. Like Kyle in high school (see the introduction), we could throw a better party that disrupts politics-as-usual.

Resist the temptation to choose friendships, small groups,

and churches based on political affinity. Refuse to cut certain people out of your life or slowly drift away from relationships because of someone leaning differently. Rather than being carried away by the cultural currents of division, swim toward your brothers and sisters in Christ.

So, who's at your table? Do you have meaningful relationships with followers of Jesus who see the world differently from you? When you think of your meals with others over this past season, can you identify at least one person from each of the four quadrants?

Meals are powerful. There's something about food that affirms relationship. Every election season, you could make a list of people you're likely to avoid because of their perspective and set up a meal with them. You don't have to talk about politics. Merely being together and reaffirming the relationship is a powerful countercultural witness to Jesus.

If the conversation turns political, seek to understand more than to be understood. Ask good questions. Why do they care so deeply? Are they angry, afraid, confused? What information sources are they drawing from? How have their life experiences shaped their convictions? How do their faith and God's Word shape their perspective? Make it your goal to understand their position so well that you could repeat it back to them in an even more compelling way than they said it. Enter these conversations prayerfully and with a determination to assume the best of them.

You might be saying, *Yeah, but it's just so uncomfortable to be with those people.* Discomfort can be a catalyst for good! You need them; they need you, too. Let the uncomfortable conversations be the very place you meet with Jesus together. Commit to relationship. Share hundreds of meals with brothers and sisters in Christ who lean in different directions. Anticipate the party of the King. Invite the world to his great feast.

PRAYER

"God, please make my candidate win." Perhaps this prayer sounds familiar. We tend to reduce God to a cosmic lobbyist, if we pray about politics at all, recruiting him for our camp. Scripture gives a much richer vision of prayer, however, where God is the ruler of creation, who invites us into *his* purposes—including politically—for the world.

We are to pray "for kings and all those in authority."[14] Notice Paul didn't qualify this with "if they're in your political party." In context, this was for the Roman Empire, who was persecuting the church. If anyone had an excuse to pray *against* their leaders, it was the early church. Yet Paul said to pray *for* them.

Can you pray for presidents who are on the other side? Can you pray for their good and guidance, not just their downfall or for them to be replaced? Can you break through the walls of hostility and crash their party with prayer?

Consider using your ballot as a prayer guide. It provides the names of candidates to pray for. Often, it's easy to see them as simply talking heads rather than real people made in God's image. Many treat them as either saviors or demons. We need to pray that the praise won't go to their heads and the critique won't go to their hearts. Don't vilify leaders you disagree with or label them as categorically evil. That's a common temptation today, but we must remember they're made in the image of God.

Pray for them.

Leaders face overwhelming stress and pressure. Pray for their spiritual, physical, and mental health. Pray for their families, who can suffer from their absence in campaign seasons or from the onslaught of attack ads and threatening letters. Pray they will not compromise their convictions for power or money or succumb to cynicism with their limited capacity to effect real change.

Your ballot can also highlight pain points in your community. Rather than just voting on a ballot measure about education, take time to pray for the teachers, students, and administrators in your community. Paul also told us *how* to pray, with "petitions, prayers, intercession and thanksgiving [being] made for all people."[15] Notice that: *all* people.

You might hesitate to pray for political things because it doesn't sound very spiritual and you don't want to treat God as your cosmic lobbyist. But there's another danger here: You might treat God instead as your personalized therapist, who helps you live your best life but is uninvolved in the grit of the real world around you.

We'll thank God for our daily bread but not for the farmers, truckers, and Department of Transportation who grow it, deliver it, and ensure we have paved roads to bring it to us. We'll pray for the health of those we love but not for the doctors, nurses, hospitals, research facilities, good water policy, and Department of Sanitation promoting health in our community.

Don't settle for a truncated prayer life; pray for God's world.

Our political prayers should be less about getting God on our side and more about making sure we are on his side. More about coming into his presence, realigning our priorities, and seeking his purposes in the world.

Jesus taught us to pray, "Your kingdom come, your will be done."[16] Consider reimagining news headlines around the inbreaking of God's kingdom. After reading about bombings in Syria, for example, my friend Jim prayed that Aleppo would become the ultimate vacation destination, so safe that people would nap in the streets and party at night. When he saw a news story about a shortage of virologists to fight an epidemic, he prayed that they would no longer be needed because Jesus had eliminated all viruses, with vacant hospitals turned into museums celebrating the healing brought by him.

You can do this too. Take a news headline, imagine what it would be like without the sin and suffering that torment our world, and use it as a prayer prompt to bring before the King. Such a practice can turn our cynical engagement with the news into a rich time in God's presence, trading an anxious search for political saviors for a cultivated longing for Jesus's kingdom.

SILENCE, SOLITUDE, AND FASTING

We often relate fasting with not eating, but we can fast from more than food. During the last election season, we invited our church to fast from social media for the forty days leading up to Election Day. We figured people had already generally made up their minds about how they were voting and that much of the online conversation would be marked by unfruitful bitterness and bickering. We encouraged people to use the extra time to pray for the flourishing of their neighbors and to have face-to-face conversations.

Many people experienced a palpable sense of peace and deep connection with others during a nationally contentious season. Some friends were so affected that they never signed back on to social media!

A few people criticized this as a withdrawal from "the real world." The irony, however, is that social media is *not* the real world. We've learned, in the years since that election, that the most heated arguments on social media are often instigated by bots or content generated by "troll factories" in countries that want to destabilize American life. And it has worked. Fake articles tear apart real relationships.

Social media is not the real world; it's a highly curated medium that uses insights from neuroscience to create algorithms that accelerate sensational content so it can capture our attention and sell it to advertisers. It's a business, and guess what?

You're the product.

One day, two friends in our church who had drastically different political leanings did a little experiment. They wanted to find common ground but were both baffled by "false information" the other was promoting. So they compared their Facebook feeds. It was jarring to see the contrast. Each feed filtered a stream of news stories that not only confirmed their own bias but also contained the most extreme caricatures of the other side.

Neither could be called "reality."

The real world is where we share real meals with real humans and have real conversations that include real body language and a real tone of voice. That's the perfect setting to engage real issues and cry out to a real God to intervene. Social media has a place, but when we practice fasting from it, we're not stepping away from reality; we are creating space to reconnect with it.

God is the true foundation of reality. The goal of fasting is to encounter him. We eliminate something from our lives to cultivate a deeper hunger for him. Fasting from food is still important, but we can also fast from the noise in our information-saturated world. We can allow the good news of his kingdom to crash through the commotion and clanging that surround us. We can turn down the volume of pundits to make space for the Prince of Peace.

You might also consider a fast from giving unsolicited opinions. My friend Luke admits that he has a tendency to talk a lot and can dominate conversations. When a friend confronted him on this, Luke undertook a weeklong fast where he only asked questions and refrained from giving his opinion unless specifically asked. He says it was amazing. The conversations were deep; he walked away feeling more connected to the people.

Ironically, many of these conversations ended in tears as people shared their deepest hearts.

I want to get better at listening. People want to be known, but sometimes I don't make space for that. I can care more about making a point than making a difference. Asking questions and sincerely listening prioritizes high-quality relationships over my own opinions. If you struggle with being argumentative over politics, you might consider committing to a season of fasting from giving your opinion and instead asking good questions. It's a great party-conversation trick.

Silence and solitude are also powerful. I love taking nightly walks to pour out my heart to God. To silence the noise of my day and listen for the voice of my heavenly Father. To create space from others and be present to Jesus. When dealing with conflict, political or otherwise, this is a great way to re-center on the King. When other things are competing for your attention, create space to make Jesus great again. And prioritize your formation in the values of his kingdom.

* * *

The church *is* political. It's not just about how we vote or what we post on social media; it's about the kind of citizens we're becoming. Traditional Christian practices are designed to form us—if we allow them to—into a particular kind of people. Worshipping God together comes with an invitation to pledge our ultimate allegiance to a better party. Our gathered and scattered practices should shape us into the image of Jesus as citizens of his kingdom.

What about actual political engagement, you might be asking, *in the traditional sense?* Great question. It's to this that we now turn.

Reflection Questions

- How do you consume information on a daily basis? What are your go-to sources for news and entertainment? How do those sources compare to your rhythms of engaging Scripture? Which way of obtaining information carries more weight? Do you find yourself quoting articles or social media posts more frequently than Scripture when justifying your perspective to others?

- Take your phone and scroll through the last ten to twenty text-message threads. Can you identify at least one person from each of the quadrants? If not, how might you pursue relationship with those with different leanings? Ask God to bring to mind the people with whom you need to share a meal.

- Have you ever experienced being part of a group or community where everyone has the same political perspective? What was that experience like? Did it lead to a more extreme perspective on certain issues?

- What political issues do you tend to talk about most? How often do you bring those to God in prayer? What are your biggest barriers to praying about public issues?

- What's the smallest change to your daily rhythms that would have the biggest impact on your life?

CREATIVE OPTIONS FOR POLITICAL INVOLVEMENT

You might think there are only three options for political involvement:

- *The Elephant Option:* Pledge your full allegiance to the Republican Party and enthusiastically support anything it does.
- *The Donkey Option:* Pledge your full allegiance to the Democratic Party and enthusiastically support anything it does.
- *The Ostrich Option:* Bury your head in the sand and hope it all blows over.

None of these are faithful Christian witness.

Fortunately, you have many more options. In this chapter, I want to "break the box" and offer you six creative options for political involvement.[1] This list is not exhaustive, yet each of the options is rooted in ancient wisdom from the Christian tradition. The goal is to expand our imaginations for what Christian political witness might look like.

You can draw on ancient wisdom to build a better future.

THE LOCAL OPTION

My friend Jim shared a recent conversation he had with Andy over lunch at Princess Market (shout-out to a favorite local Middle Eastern restaurant!). Their conversation on foreign policy meandered through half a dozen topics, like Iran's nuclear capacity, the ethics of drone warfare, the Lebanese economy, and the role of nationalism in Turkey's last coup attempt. Jim confessed he was emotionally charged because Andy challenged some strong convictions of his. But Andy also made a warm statement to affirm their friendship despite disagreement.

As they poked at the last few pieces of baklava, Andy said something that changed Jim: "It's fun to have conversations about the Middle East, though we can't really do anything about it. Yet most people couldn't name the members of their local city council." Jim chuckled in nervous agreement, he said, to hide a sinking feeling. "I'd spent the last two hours pontificating about peace in the Middle East but had no clear vision for how to seek the peace of Tempe, my own city. I was name-dropping the head of Turkey's Cumhuriyet Party, yet I was one of those people who could not name a single member of my local government. Not. A. Single. One."

Jim's not alone; I've historically not known many of mine, either!

The Local Option emphasizes local involvement over the national (and international). When Americans think politics, we tend to focus on the "big" things in D.C.: the presidential election, debates in Congress, and seats on the Supreme Court. Those things are important, but the sad reality is that most people can have only a minuscule impact there. Rather than spending the bulk of our time and energy shouting into the void on such issues, we instead can have a significant impact locally.

There's a rich Christian history of prioritizing the local. *Subsidiarity*, for example, is a core tenet in much Christian social teaching (particularly in the Catholic tradition), which holds that issues should be dealt with at the most local or immediate level possible. "A central authority should have a subsidiary function, performing only those tasks which cannot be performed at a more local level."[2] In other words, if something can be done by a decentralized entity closer to the ground, it should be.

While federal and state governments have important roles to play in the common good, subsidiarity focuses on the currency of local relationships and knowledge in families, churches, voluntary communities, and local governments before seeking intervention from larger, distant entities. At a local level, we often better understand the unique issues our particular communities face, can dream up more creative ideas for our context, and form stronger relationships to collaborate for the good of our neighbors.

The average person can also have a bigger practical impact. Our voices are amplified when engaging locally. One person I know lost an election for city council in Burlington, Vermont, by a mere thirty-two votes. (I had that many people at a house party!) While a social media post about Biden or Trump is basically a drop in the bucket, a few people could have a profound impact in Burlington with a couple of media posts. An informed vote carries weight in local communities.

You can also advocate for good policies more effectively. We saw this when the predatory lending industry tried to pass a bill in Arizona that would have allowed extremely high interest rates (such as a 204 percent APR over 24 months!) in loans to the working poor.[3] This would have exploited our local brothers and sisters, so churches rallied to their defense.

A local network of churches we're part of got involved. Churches were called to pray. More than thirty-five churches sent a letter asking state senators to reject the bill. Pastors met with lawmakers in person, many of whom were in their churches. The network knew the negative effect this could have—because many church leaders ministered in poor areas—and was in relationship with those who could be impacted most.

It worked. The bill was rejected, which likely kept the working poor in our community from sinking into insurmountable debt. Jesus's people were able to crash through a political agenda that was dangerous for our neighbors. Our collective voices were heard because we had real relationships rooted in a local community.

Your voice and vote can have a significant local influence. Since the overturning of *Roe v. Wade,* your state legislature will have substantially more impact on unborn children than will the stated position of any presidential candidate. Affordable housing can be more influenced by local decisions than by discussions hundreds of miles away at the Department of Housing and Urban Development.

Our city, county, and state leaders are often desperate for constituents to engage in local issues. Yet city council meetings, bills in the state legislature, and school board discussions are met with shrugs of apathy. Do you know the names of your local city council members? Or your representatives in the state legislature? Or the legislative district in which you live and the most important issues in your community?

Local leaders are asking for our voices. We're often encouraged to call our national legislators to advocate for policies, and that's fine. But your state legislators and city government leaders are much more likely to pay attention to your voice and even more likely to meet with you.

If you find yourself yelling into the abyss on social media to family and friends whose minds you probably won't be able to change, the question you should ask is, *Do I want to make a point, or do I want to make a difference?*

Prioritize the local. Focus on small over big. You can have a greater impact on the flourishing of your neighbors. You can join whichever party you're in and make it better on the ground. Your vote and your voice are often more fruitful when rooted in your community.

Sure, vote national, but work local.

THE DANIEL OPTION

There are politicians in our churches. People who work on city council, in the state legislature, or in the national office. The Daniel Option is for those called to work in political office or more directly in the political process.

Daniel is an important figure in the Bible who worked in the heights of Babylon's government. God used his faithful presence there in powerful ways. There's much we can learn from Daniel. First, he had to exercise discernment. Upon entering Babylon, he refused to eat meat from the king's table but let the Babylonians rename him after a foreign god. (I'd be saying, *C'mon, Daniel! Take the steak, but don't let them name you after a pagan god.*)[4] The Bible doesn't say why he did that; scholars are divided. Yet Scripture commends his wisdom.

We need to give space and grace for those in political office to navigate difficult decisions. Politics is the art of compromise, and there may be times when a politician must make compromises to work with others toward a bigger picture. That's not to say they should violate their conscience or cave to bribery or corruption, but there are often gray areas that require wisdom and discernment before God.

Next, Daniel's ultimate allegiance was to God. He refused to bow to the idols of Babylon (and was famously thrown in the lions' den for it!). He knew Babylon was a pagan power, fueled by ideologies opposed to God. Although he exercised discernment, there were lines he refused to cross.

In our day, you won't stare down the mouth of a lion for resisting idolatry, but you could face a stream of insults from the ferocious mouths of people you thought were friends. Faithful Christians in the Democratic Party are called bigots for not embracing their party's ideas around sexuality. Faithful Christians in the Republican Party are called RINOs (Republican In Name Only) or "woke snowflakes" for challenging racism. It's okay to be a member of a party; just know that the party is embedded in an idolatrous system that can push on you when you resist.

There's wisdom here from the Reformed tradition. Abraham Kuyper was a politician (as well as a theologian, pastor, educator, and journalist) who served as prime minister of the Netherlands from 1901 to 1905. He once said,

> There is not a square inch in the whole domain of our human existence over which Christ, who is Sovereign over all, does not cry: "Mine!"[5]

That statement speaks to the heart of Reformed political engagement, which emphasizes God's sovereign rule over all of life. There is no sacred/secular divide. Everything belongs to Jesus. Including politics.

This is often called "sphere sovereignty"—the idea is that God is King *over* each sphere of society: government, business, education, health care, media, the arts, the church, and more. Each sphere has its own purpose and limited scope of responsibility. Society functions best when each sphere "stays in its lane," without interfering in matters that belong to another sphere.

God is King over families, for example, who are responsible for the formation and protection of children. God is King over the government, which is responsible for public justice. God is King over the church, which is responsible for making disciples through the ministry of Word and Spirit.

This is important, because it keeps the church from trying to take over the government and institute a theocracy. Christians can seek to keep the government accountable to its particular role of protecting and promoting public justice, without trying to use it to make people Christians (which is the role of the church, given different tools for the task).

With this mindset, Christians can enter political office or join a political party and pursue policy for the flourishing of our neighbors. We can do so with a humble and hardworking posture while recognizing there are limits to what the government can or should do.

The Daniel Option involves rooting yourself in a particular political party or movement to seek the flourishing of your neighbors while not giving your full allegiance to that party. You're a party crasher like Daniel, entering the party and working from the inside but refusing to conform to the partisan scripts and pressures that surround you. This is a hard path because you will be entering an idolatrous system that will seek your ultimate allegiance.

At a minimum, this will mean being well informed to advocate for policies that—to the best of your knowledge—will genuinely make the world better. It can mean supporting, volunteering for, or donating to candidates who display the most integrity. It could mean taking some unpopular positions at times.

You might even consider running for local office. It may not be as far-fetched as it seems, especially if you're willing to run for something more obscure. Offices such as constable and corporation commission rarely get press but have significant impacts on people's lives. You might also consider joining a local board or committee or find nongovernmental ways to contribute to civic flourishing.

If you do run for office, your character matters. You'll need to resist toxic tactics like slandering your opponents or pandering to special interests, however common these strategies might be in our culture. As Martin Luther King, Jr., says, "The means we use must be as pure as the ends we seek."[6] Don't lose your soul to avoid losing your campaign. Faithfulness matters.

Our final lesson from Daniel is that he knew where his true home was. He prayed daily facing Jerusalem.[7] Though he served in Babylon, his true citizenship was in God's city. Similarly, Christians working in politics should seek God's wisdom in prayer, fueled by a posture of dependence, knowing our higher citizenship is hidden in Christ with God.

Some think politics is too corrupt for Christians to be meaningfully involved in. Yet figures like Daniel in Babylon and Joseph in Egypt give us biblical role models for that courageous space of high-level leadership within idolatrous systems. It will involve wrestling with complex ethical issues, sometimes making pragmatic concessions, and other times drawing the line to challenge an unjust culture.

The Daniel Option can be a difficult path. Yet for those with soft hearts and steel spines, it can be a faithful way of serving God's world.

THE PROPHETIC OPTION

When Martin Luther King, Jr., delivered his famous "I Have a Dream" speech at the historic march on Washington, D.C., he was joined by about 250,000 people hungry for a different future. While he did not hold political office, he spoke with prophetic power that crashed through the status quo. The movement he led had endured attacks with dogs and fire hoses, slanderous verbal assaults, and arrests with time in jail. Yet its prophetic imagination made a new reality seem possible.

If the Daniel Option works from within the system, the Prophetic Option seeks to bring change from outside the system. There is much wisdom here from the black church and civil rights movement. Their supporters frequently did not hold positions of power, yet they engaged in nonviolent action that exposed injustice and opened up new possibilities for the future.

The prophetic imagination challenges the rules of the game. It confronts the existing plausibility structure to make a new future seem possible.

What might a new party look like whose goal was not so much to win as to reshape our political imagination for the future? Few people knew what libertarianism was before Ron Paul's campaign. Bernie Sanders created the plausibility structure for socialists to win local elections. Is there an opportunity for a similar movement, inspired by Christ?

For fun, let's call our movement the Prophetic Loser Party (since we know we won't win). A group of Christians (like you and your friends) could come together to form a political community. Rather than focus on national issues, you'd have candidates run for local offices like city council or a school board. You'd have people who lean left and right and are committed to a platform of things, like the following:

- *Love of Neighbor:* motivated by the self-giving love of Christ rather than the self-interested love of money and power; amplifying the voice of the vulnerable more than the voice of the highest bidder.

- *All of Life:* caring for the whole scope of life in God's world; refusing to polarize between economics and the environment, young mothers and unborn children, national security and national hospitality, justice and peace.

- *Fruitful Speech:* engaging in political discourse that displays the fruit of the Spirit; combining deep conviction with generous civility.

- *Local Collaboration:* respecting and partnering with people on the Right and the Left while refusing to be owned by the idols of either party; focusing on local action more than on national speculation.

- *Faithful Witness:* valuing faithful witness over winning, with the highest priority to leave the community with a better picture of Jesus.

Instead of trashing our political opponents, what if we publicly praised their accomplishments on social media in areas of common ground? Instead of ignoring outside counsel, what if we were known as the best listeners in political history? Instead of promoting fear of refugees or mocking disabled people, what if we included them on our advisory boards?

This party could include practices like these:

- *A Quarterly Failure Report:* Instead of constant boasting about our successes, we could publish a report that honestly acknowledged the ways we've failed to meet our promises or serve the community.

- *A Listening Bus:* The bus would drive around town with candidates on board. Anyone in the city could get on the bus and explain their perspective on the state's problems to the candidate. There's one major rule on this bus: The candidates can only ask questions.

- *Campaigning Together:* Candidates who lean in different directions could campaign together, modeling respectful disagreement with fruitful speech and promoting a different spirit of civil discourse.

- *Voice to the Voiceless:* An advisory board could consist of both the powerless and the powerful (blue-collar and white-collar, schoolteachers and refugees, stay-at-home parents and small-business owners, religious and ethnic minorities, college students and even people who belong to opposing political parties). The goal would be to represent the actual people we are called to serve, not just those with power.

- *A Respect Report:* During each election, the alliance could write a paper outlining the achievements, good policies, and competencies of political opponents. It would be a tool to acknowledge their dignity and our shared commitment to the common good.

Recent politicians have stood out with shocking words and outlandish behavior. The Prophetic Loser Party could also stand out with absurd antics, only it would be the absurdity of integrity and love. A movement based on absurd love just might garner free media attention and social media buzz, allowing it to run on the currency of creativity rather than money with strings attached. It might actually provide a better party.

As a pastor, I'm not in a place to launch something like this (my own sphere is keeping me plenty busy!). But maybe it will spark your imagination and inspire you to challenge the rules of the game with creative action that paints the possibility of a different political future.

THE SCUBA OPTION

Jenny is an advocate for families with special-needs children. Her organization has served more than three thousand children in foster care. She's a member of our church who pours out tear-filled prayers for young girls who've been sexually abused or victims of trafficking. She works tirelessly to make sure countless little boys don't wind up in the school-to-prison pipeline. She's skilled at navigating complex systems and bureaucracies.

Jenny is a prime example of the Scuba Option, someone who dives deep to become an expert in a particular area. You might feel pressure to become an expert in every area of politics, but that's really not possible and the ability to have a positive influence with shallow facts and cliché slogans is minimal. So, just as a scuba diver isn't content to snorkel around broadly on the surface, people like Jenny see the power of going deep in a particular area, exploring the complexities and nuances of the issue to advocate for meaningful change.

Ancient wisdom is found here in heroes like William Wilberforce, who fought for the abolition of slavery in England. He worked tirelessly for forty-six years, driven by his allegiance to Jesus. It was only on his deathbed, three days before he passed, that he learned that his life's work had succeeded in abolishing slavery in most of the British Empire.

He dove deep for decades.

So, where do you begin? The Scuba Option often starts with your own story. For Jenny, it began when her daughter was diagnosed with autism. Jenny navigated dozens of visits with speech therapists, occupational therapists, and child psychologists. They all agreed her daughter needed early intervention and a good educational program. The only problem was that these services were hard to get into and way more expensive than their family could afford.

Driven by love for her daughter, Jenny threw herself into the world of education, special needs, and funding for developmental services. She persevered through red tape, stacks of forms, hundreds of phone calls, and sleepless nights with her daughter waking up at 2 A.M.

Other families sought Jenny out. She had developed a deep understanding of the resources and systems available for children with disabilities. She was happy to help and soon became an educational advocate.

Is there an issue God has prepared you for? You might feel haunted by the question *What's the most important issue?* The options can seem overwhelming. You can spend years reflecting on what you *should* do and never end up doing anything. Perhaps a better question comes from author Steve Garber, who invites us to ask, "Knowing what I know, what will I do?"[8] In other words, *How has my life experience prepared me to contribute?*

If you've struggled with learning disabilities, you might be one of the most equipped to dive deep into education policy. The best people to focus on criminal justice might be those who grew up with an incarcerated parent. Maybe your work as a hydrologist has prepared you to focus on water policy. Perhaps the tears a mother sheds, upon receiving news of her daughter's diagnosis, are an invitation to follow Jesus into the deep pain of children in her city.

This "scuba work" often requires sacrifice. Jenny was well paid, but something didn't sit right. She realized only wealthy families could afford her services. Her heart broke for low-income families who could not hire her, or foster children who bounced from home to home. Who would advocate for them? She sensed God calling her to step down from her well-paying job to start a nonprofit. There was a risk, but it was inspired by sacrificial love, and it paid off.

The Scuba Option is not glamorous. It's often about reading bills, tracing root causes, and volunteering in uncelebrated obscurity. It's building relationships with those who can make a difference and advocating for good policy, even when the problem is not a hot-button issue. English novelist George Eliot puts it well:

> The growing good of the world is partly dependent on unhistoric acts; and that things are not so ill with you and me as they might have been, is half owing to the number who lived faithfully a hidden life, and rest in unvisited tombs.[9]

In other words, God uses people willing to focus on the uncelebrated, overlooked, unpopular work to sustain our lives in crucial ways. Like a potluck, God's party relies on quiet contributions from a wide variety of people who together make things better. You can be one of those people, hidden in Christ.

The Scuba Option is more political than it sometimes looks. Even though Jenny doesn't focus on public policy, her voice is sought out by elected officials, think tanks, and decision-makers for governmental departments. She speaks into policies and procedures to prevent abuse and homelessness and provide special-education services. While many people talk and post about sex trafficking and criminal justice, she has put in the hidden work that has made not only a point but a difference.

Many people in our city tell tear-filled stories of how Jenny reflects the self-giving love of Jesus, showing up for a kid in need. Her impact came not from an abundance of money or power but rather from a willingness to work hard in one area.

She dove deep; you can too.

THE MONASTIC OPTION

The poor monks are often misunderstood. Some people think of monastic communities as fearfully withdrawing from society, leaving the neighborhood party, and becoming so heavenly minded as to be no earthly good. Yet they were actually focused on transforming a corrupt society by forming an alternative community within it, throwing a better party from the inside, with arms stretched toward the outside, and cultivating the ground beneath their feet.

Their agriculture, construction, and scholarship transformed Europe. Theologian John Henry Newman describes their good work: "They found a swamp, a moor, a thicket, a rock, and they made an Eden in the wilderness."[10] As the missiologist David Bosch observes,

> Even secular historians acknowledge that the agricultural restoration of the largest part of Europe has to be attributed to them. Through their disciplined and tireless labor they turned the tide of barbarism in Western Europe and brought back into cultivation the lands which had been deserted and depopulated in the age of the invasions. More

important, through their sanctifying work and poverty they lifted the hearts of the poor and neglected peasants and inspired them while at the same time revolutionizing the order of social values which had dominated the empire's slave-owning society.[11]

Monastic communities addressed poverty, community development, education, national security, and environmental stewardship—all without holding governmental positions.

The Monastic Option is about more than becoming a monk. I'm using it here to describe forming an alternative community in the midst of the empire. There is historic wisdom here in the Anabaptist tradition, which has emphasized that the primary purpose of the church is not to change the world but to *be* the church.[12] It is through our shared life together, as an outpost of the kingdom, that we are able to most effectively transform the world around us.

This is a great option for many of us. Maybe you're frustrated by politics and looking for another way to contribute. Maybe you can't enter the political space without being compromised. Maybe the aforementioned options don't fit the opportunities in front of you. Maybe you're overwhelmed by the decay in society and looking for a way to plant something new.

You can hunker down. Not in isolation but rather contributing to the shared life of a local church. You can cultivate a countercultural community who lives together under the reign of Jesus. You can have a political impact—like the monks—without being directly involved in politics.

This is Norah from our church, who leads a team of volunteers to support teen moms through our YoungLives partnership, which has helped these women flourish and feel they don't have to choose an abortion. This is Lucas and Sabrina from our church, who turned their carport into an affordable studio apartment and deliberately chose not to put it on Airbnb, because they care about affordable housing and wanted to make another unit available without contributing to skyrocketing rent prices. This is Monica from our church, who coaches Somali teens and does dinner-table diplomacy with them as she mentors and shares meals around her table each week.

I could share dozens more examples.

We can influence almost any political issue outside the realm of traditional politics. When we plant deep roots as a local church, we can grow abundant fruit in our community—like the monks do. We can become a microcosm of what God's reign looks like, bearing witness to a better party, on earth as in heaven.

THE REFORM OPTION

One final option. What if the national hot-button issues are not the most significant problems we face but rather symptoms of a deeper disease? What if their visible rash points to an underlying illness deep in the bones of the American political system? A sickness that causes pain throughout our whole social body?

We know that politics is broken. We all know that it's driven by financial influence. That we're stuck with only two parties to choose from. That those parties are producing increasingly extreme candidates. Some of us may need to take the Reform Option. This option shifts our focus from specific issues to addressing underlying problems with the system.

Many people would act if they just knew how. Here are a few examples to consider. This isn't an exhaustive list, and I'm not proposing these as policies you must embrace, but I want to spark your imagination with some possible ways to reform the system.

First, *ranked-choice voting*. This voting process would allow you to rank candidates rather than simply choose one.[13]
Why is this important? Consider this silly example to illustrate
how our current system incentivizes the most extreme candidates.

Imagine Captain America, Wonder Woman, Superman, and
Thanos are all running for president.[14] Thanos is running on a
radical platform of population control by collecting infinity
stones to snap his fingers and eliminate half the population. He
has a small but passionate group of devoted followers who want
him to direct government resources toward finding those stones.
About 70 percent of the population is against this policy and
adamant that Thanos should never be in office.

The problem is that Captain America, Wonder Woman, and
Superman all have a similar platform of seeking a safe and just
society. Most voters want these three *way* more than they want
Thanos but are unsure who to choose. In our single-choice system, here are the results:

> Thanos: 30%
> Wonder Woman: 28%
> Superman: 22%
> Captain America: 20%

Thanos wins, snaps his fingers, and makes half the world dis-
appear. Party over.

What happened? Superman, Wonder Woman, and Captain
America split the vote, even though Thanos was the last choice
for the vast majority of the population.

Our single-choice system often ends up splitting the vote—
especially in the primaries—between a number of similar, more
reasonable candidates. Extreme candidates may have only a

small percentage of votes but end up with a higher percentage than the other candidates. The split can crash the system. After the primaries, many of us often feel like we're stuck choosing between the lesser of two evils.

With ranked-choice voting, you rank candidates on the ballot by preference rather than choosing only one. In our silly example, Wonder Woman would have won because she was the first or second choice for a majority of the population.[15] It's a little more complicated than that, but the main point is this would help prevent the most extreme and inflammatory candidates from being elected. This could produce more high-character and better-qualified candidates who appeal to the broadest number of people.

Another reform measure to consider is *proportional representation*. Our districts face the problem of winner-take-all elections. Let's say your district, for example, has a vote of 50 percent Democrat, 40 percent Republican, and 10 percent Other Party; in that case, the Democrats alone win a seat in Congress. Proportional representation, however, would use the state as a whole, or at least much larger voting districts, and—assuming for the sake of example the same voting percentage breakdown with ten seats available—the number of seats in Congress would look like this:

> Democrats: 5 seats
> Republicans: 4 seats
> Other Party: 1 seat

This would allow smaller parties to emerge and functionally play a tiebreaker role in a gridlocked Congress. With just 10 percent of the vote, in our example above, a third party would have representation.

This could help address a major problem with our system: We're essentially stuck choosing between two parties. The quiet majority of Christians feel increasingly politically homeless because they don't fit squarely into a political party. Or, at least, they wish there were better options. Proportional representation could help break up the two-party system with some healthy competition.

What if there were truly more options to choose from? Could that contribute to healthier options? Could it incentivize the Democratic and Republican parties to compete by putting forward healthier options of their own? Could it make each one a better party?

Instead of carving a state into gerrymandered congressional districts, you treat the state as a whole (or at least larger districts) and vote for a particular party. That party puts forward a ranked list of their best candidates and then wins seats in proportion to the percentage of votes they receive. This would break the duopoly and allow new parties to emerge.

These are just two examples of ways to reform the system. There are others as well, like campaign-finance reform, single-ballot primaries, and term limits. The point in mentioning these is not to say they'd change everything, but to say they could play enormous roles in creating a healthier political system. There may be problems with such examples, too, but I wanted to highlight some ways people are working to reform the system that could contribute to an improved political culture.

The Reform Option can also provide an opportunity for us to work with others across party lines whom we might otherwise have significant disagreements with, crashing through traditional barriers to together reform the system and seek the flourishing of our communities.

*   *   *

So, we have more options than the Elephant, the Donkey, and the Ostrich. My hope has been to expand your imagination by offering a broader array of alternatives for what a faithful political witness might look like. Though these six options are different, they are all united.

Under the party of the Lamb.

Reflection Questions

- Which of the six options resonated with you the most? Why do you think that approach stands out to you?

- Which of the six options would be most challenging for you to take? Why?

- Spend some time in prayer to see if you sense an invitation to move forward with one of the options. What are the first few steps you would need to take?

- Read through the list of creative options and try to identify at least one friend who would thrive with each of the approaches. Consider sending them a note of encouragement regarding the gifts and abilities you see in them or sharing an insight from this book with them.

CONCLUSION

A Better Party

Kyle threw a better party. Back in high school, he not only crashed parties, disrupted cliques, and overcame divides, but he also threw epic celebrations we all wanted to be at. Similarly, Jesus throws a better party. His goal is not simply to disrupt the status quo but to call us into something greater.

Jesus invites unexpected people to his party. All through the Gospels, people attack Jesus for the crowd he feasts with: tax collectors and sinners. Today, our society cares less about *moral* uprightness ("tax collectors and sinners")[1] and more about *political* rightness (Fox News or CNN). Partisan ideology *is* the new morality. You won't get canceled for hanging out with "naughty" people, but you might for inviting the other side of the aisle to the table.

Here's the thing: Jesus doesn't care! He's more focused on the kingdom celebration than on the critics and naysayers. That is how you can gain confidence to overcome our partisan divide: You focus on Jesus and press into his kingdom.

It will be hard. There will be resistance. There may have been a day when you could coast along in your party without compromising the fruit of the Spirit, but that day is not today. Like for Daniel in Babylon, the heat in the pressure cooker has been turned up. Like for Shadrach, Meshach, and Abednego, refusing to submit to the idols might get you roasted. But don't convert to the political religions. Their idols and ideologies offer a false vision of salvation that ultimately will not satisfy. You need to press deeper into your life with God to stand strong under the pressure.

Are you a party crasher? That's the question I want to leave you with. Will you be a party crasher, like Jesus? Will you resist conforming to the partisan boxes and scripts of our culture in order to pledge your ultimate allegiance to the King of kings?

Jesus is worth it. His kingdom is greater; his party is better. Faithfulness to him is worth everything. He's inviting you to bring your lean but submit your bow, pledging your ultimate allegiance to him. He's inviting you to his feast, to a table set with bread and wine where he gives you himself. He's inviting you to eat and fellowship with others who lean in all sorts of different directions, because that's part of the point. (Union with Christ means union with his body—the body of Christ—in all its eclectic diversity.) He's inviting you to invite others to this strange celebration, this reconciling kingdom, this better party for the world.

Will that look strange? Yes. Will it turn heads in a partisan world? Yes. But it's worth it. Let's keep Christianity weird. Let's be like the early church, who didn't look for a middle-of-the-road path of least resistance but rather boldly held to multiple extremes at once. Let's be about multiethnic community, care for the poor, a faithful sexual ethic, the sanctity of life, radical forgiveness, and enemy love. Let's prayerfully discern where Christ is calling us to be bold in other areas of our fresh context today. And let's do so in a way that doesn't compromise the fruit of his Spirit or the integrity of our witness.

Character matters. Christ says that *how* we stand is as important as *what* we stand for. So let's follow the Ten Political Commitments. Let's place a higher priority on following Jesus than we do on winning political points. Let's resist the lie that God gave an exemption clause for our character when it comes to politics. Let's be peacemakers rather than peacefakers or peacebreakers. Let's take the logs out of our own eyes first so we can see clearly to help our brothers and sisters. Let's take the high road and be known as enemy-loving, fruit-of-the-Spirit-bearing, laying-down-our-lives-for-our-neighbors reconcilers who follow the Servant King and the God of Peace.

God, give us soft hearts and steel spines.

Jesus is throwing a better party. And you're invited. There's a toast I like to give at parties—at least parties with friends who follow Jesus. We raise our glasses around the table and together declare, "To the King and the kingdom." If you're a follower of Jesus, I want to end this book by similarly inviting you to raise your glass to the party of the Lamb, around a table big enough to redeem our partisan divide, with the bread of his body given and wine of his blood shed, our exalted and reigning King. Let us declare together, through our words and our lives, our pledge of allegiance to him.

To the King and the kingdom.

DISCUSSION QUESTIONS

CHAPTER 1: THE FOUR POLITICAL RELIGIONS

1. How do political ideologies compare with historic world religions in terms of devotion and conversion?

2. How does this framework help you understand your experiences during past election seasons?

3. Reflect on each of the political religions one by one. Imagine how the world would change if everyone converted to that political religion.

    - What would change?
    - Who would benefit?
    - Who might suffer?

4. Not only do the four quadrants create false gods, but they also create false devils. Specific people or issues are treated as the primary source of evil. Who or what are the false devils created by each quadrant?

5. How can we as God's people navigate the four quadrants and remain faithful without giving our full allegiance?

6. What does it look like to be a church where people lean in different directions but refuse to bow to the political idols?

7. How would forming a common table during the next election season reflect the character and teaching of Jesus to a watching world?

CHAPTER 2: PLEDGING ALLEGIANCE TO THE KING OF KINGS

1. How does the concept of the sacred/secular divide negatively influence our understanding of the gospel's relevance to politics and culture?

2. What are some potential consequences of keeping Jesus confined to the "sacred" box and not letting him influence the so-called secular aspects of life?

3. What are some signs that your interest in politics has shifted from a lean to a bow?

4. How would you respond to someone who said, "Why should we even talk about politics? Shouldn't we just focus on spiritual things?"

5. Since each of the four quadrants reflects some aspect of God's creational design and is occupied by people who are made in his image, each quadrant will contain good gifts that should be affirmed. Spend some time identifying the good aspects of each quadrant and thanking God for those gifts. Try to go beyond the examples we named in the chapter.

6. Since each quadrant has been affected by the Fall, they all contain some very destructive features. Identify the sinful and broken aspects of each quadrant and pray for God to rescue people from the tyranny of idolatry.

7. What are some examples of modern-day idols that require sacrifice? What are some specific sacrifices that each political idol demands?

8. How does political idolatry affect the witness of the church?

CHAPTER 3: WELCOME TO THE KING'S TABLE

1. Imagine three different political conversations between Simon (the revolutionary Zealot) and Matthew (the tax collector). What might those conversations have sounded like? How might their conversations have changed over time?

   - Conversation 1: before they met Jesus
   - Conversation 2: around the campfire as they followed Jesus
   - Conversation 3: a week after Pentecost

2. If you could seek advice from Simon (the revolutionary Zealot) and Matthew (the tax collector) about how to follow Jesus despite political differences, what questions would you ask them? What do you think they might say?

3. When you think about the imaginary conversations between Simon and Matthew, which of those stages—before Jesus, around the campfire, after Pentecost—most resembles the conversations you have about politics?

4. Where have you seen Christian friendships, churches, and organizations fracture along political fault lines? What were the issues? How did it happen? What are specific ways you could push against that trend?

5. I gave several questions in this chapter to help evaluate whether you are bowing to an idol rather than having a healthy lean. Walk through each of them as a group and ask God to help you answer honestly.

- Do you give more time and attention to political pundits than to the words of Scripture?
- Which quadrant do you feel the need to defend or justify? How angry do questions about that quadrant make you?
- Do you have a pattern of cutting people out of your life who disagree with your politics?
- Is there a cultural leader who moves your heart more than Jesus?

6. What are tangible ways fellow believers can help one another see the creational good within each quadrant as well as what's been broken by sin?

CHAPTER 4: TEN POLITICAL COMMANDMENTS

1. How is it possible for someone to display Christlike character in their personal life but act so differently when it comes to their conduct in the political arena? What factors contribute to this inconsistency?

2. Even if we don't experience persecution today, in what ways might full allegiance to Jesus be costly?

3. If you had the chance to speak with brothers and sisters from the global church (like Vinh) who have endured violent persecution, what wisdom do you think they might offer about how to remain faithful to Jesus in a world filled with so much idolatry?

4. How can we shift our perspective from thinking that our time, money, and influence are solely for our own benefit to recognizing that those gifts ultimately belong to God and should be reimagined as instruments of his love?

5. What's the simplest way you could love someone you know who leans toward a different quadrant? What's the most out-of-the-box way you could love them? Is there a next step toward them you want to take?

6. Have you ever felt as though someone held a dehumanizing or inaccurate view of one of your convictions? What was that experience like for you?

7. How can we recognize whether we're being shaped more by the biblical story or by propaganda (idols)?

8. When was a time when your political leanings conflicted with the teachings of the Bible? How did you reconcile that conflict?

9. How can we differentiate between unhealthy and healthy conceptions of justice? In what area are you best equipped to pursue justice in a healthy way?

10. Reflect on each of the fruits of the Spirit and discuss what political discourse might look like if it reflected one of these characteristics: love, joy, peace, patience, kindness, goodness, faithfulness, gentleness, self-control.

CHAPTER 5: BREAKERS, FAKERS, AND MAKERS

1. What associations do you have with the word *peace*? How might that affect the way you perceive the Bible's teaching on peace?

2. How is peacemaking central to the gospel, and what role does it play in the mission of Jesus and his followers?

3. Why is it important to address conflicts directly with the person involved rather than talking about them behind their back or debating with them on social media?

4. What's the difference between peacebreaking, peacefaking, and peacemaking?

5. This chapter provides four steps in the peacemaking process. Reflect on each of these steps and identify why they are important. Also, name the dangers of skipping a step.

   • Step 1: Get with God.
   • Step 2: Get together.
   • Step 3: Get help.
   • Step 4: Give the gospel.

6. Which of the four steps do you tend to skip? How has that affected your relationships?

7. Why is it important to scrutinize *our* personal sin and political leanings more than those of others?

8. What is fake boldness? What kind of fake boldness are you most tempted to engage in?

9. Can you think of a time when you addressed a conflict directly with another person? How did it go, and what did you learn from the experience?

10. How does the love and forgiveness you've received from Jesus influence the way you can extend forgiveness to others?

11. How does our heavenly Father's reputation become tied to our actions as his children, especially as it relates to peacemaking?

12. What are some tangible steps we can take today to become people who love our enemies and work toward peace?

CHAPTER 6: WHEN TO BE BOLD

1. Why do people often see prayer and action as opposing forces, especially during times of national crisis or conversation?

2. How can prayer inform and motivate action? How can action be grounded in prayer?

3. In what ways have you seen prayer and action work together effectively in the past? What are some examples where one was more dominant than the other, and how did that affect the outcome?

4. In this chapter, we outline five marks of the early church. Which of them is easiest for you to embrace? Which is most challenging?

   · Multiethnic Community
   · Care for the Poor
   · Sexual Ethic
   · Pro-Life with Children
   · Forgiveness and Enemy Love

5. Why do American Christians struggle to care for all five of these marks simultaneously? Why do we tend to gravitate toward a few of them while distancing ourselves from the others?

6. If American Christians were known for passionately pursuing each of these five marks, what would it communicate about Jesus to a watching world?

7. Why is it important for the church to take a stand on issues of race and justice? What's the cost of faithfulness in this area?

8. Why is it important for the church to take a stand on issues of sexuality and gender? What's the cost of faithfulness in this area?

9. What are other important issues for which Christians should take a stand that were not mentioned in this chapter? What's the cost of faithfulness in those areas?

10. In what ways does the strangeness of Christianity provide a beautiful witness about the character of Jesus?

CHAPTER 7: AN OUTPOST OF THE KINGDOM

1. Do you agree with the idea that attending church can be a powerful political practice? Why or why not?

2. Describe how each of the following gathered practices is a political act. Also, which of these practices is most surprising to describe as political?

   - Call to Worship
   - Confession and Lament
   - Scripture and Sermon
   - Communion and Worship
   - Baptism

3. How are the different aspects of a corporate worship gathering designed to form us into faithful people who can resist idolatry?

4. How might the political quadrants provide counterfeit versions of a church worship service? (Think of a few examples.)

5. What does it mean for America to have a national liturgy of "the crisis of the week"? How can we respond with compassion to national events without being driven by headlines?

6. How should the public reading of Scripture and the sermon shape our understanding of the world? How should it counter the false stories and help us align our lives with the biblical story?

7. How can lament be used to address and process national tragedies, such as mass shootings and natural disasters? In what ways can prayer help us respond to such events?

8. How can the experience of receiving God's forgiveness and grace through confession and lament help us extend forgiveness and grace to others, even in a polarized and divisive culture?

9. In what ways can the presence of Jesus be more powerful than our strategies, opinions, and policies?

10. How is baptism similar to and different from the Pledge of Allegiance?

CHAPTER 8: FORMATIONAL PRACTICES FOR A POLARIZED WORLD

1. Why do many Christians tend to apply spiritual disciplines like Bible reading and prayer to their personal issues but not to public life?

2. What portions of Scripture do you tend to avoid and why? Make a plan to engage those parts, ideally with someone who is drawn toward them.

3. How has Scripture been twisted at times to justify certain political ideologies? (Name a few examples.) How can a better understanding of the biblical story help to prevent this?

4. How does reading the whole Bible rather than just focusing on certain passages help guard against misuse of God's Word and provide a more balanced understanding of it?

5. How can having relationships with believers with different political leanings enhance our discipleship and deepen our understanding of God?

6. How can participating in shared meals be a powerful way to build relationships within the body of Christ?

7. How can we avoid reducing God to a cosmic lobbyist when we pray about political issues and instead seek to align our prayers with his purposes for the world?

8. Read through the news headlines and try to reimagine what those headlines might sound like in a world made new. Let this exercise guide your prayers for God's kingdom to come on earth as it is in heaven.

9. When was the last time you prayed for a politician you don't like? Do a Google search for a politician you strongly disagree with and try to learn a little bit about their family. Spend time praying for them.

10. What are some creative ways to practice fasting, solitude, and silence in our information-saturated age that make more space to be attentive to God? Do you sense the Spirit inviting you to step into any of those ways?

CHAPTER 9: CREATIVE OPTIONS FOR POLITICAL INVOLVEMENT

1. The Local Option: What are the benefits of prioritizing local politics over national politics?

2. The Daniel Option: If you had to run for political office, what office would you want to run for? Imagine that you won—how would you resist the temptation to give your full allegiance to your political party? How would you seek to remain faithful to Jesus and his ways?

3. The Prophetic Option: This section imagined a Prophetic Loser Party, which would be more focused on faithful witness than winning an election, with specific countercultural practices that this party would engage in. Which of the following ideas resonated most with you? How do you think the world would react to a candidate or political community that put that idea into practice?

   - an honest failure report that acknowledges ways a candidate has fallen short
   - a listening bus, where candidates are only allowed to ask questions
   - candidates who lean in different directions but campaign together
   - an advisory board consisting of both the powerless and the powerful
   - candidates who would regularly post things they respect about their opponent

4. The Scuba Option: If you had to dive deep into one particular issue, what would you choose? What challenges have you faced in your life that have equipped you to engage that issue?

5. The Monastic Option: In what ways does being an alternative community offer a way to love your neighbor without compromising your convictions?

6. The Reform Option: If you could change one aspect of our political system or processes, what would you change? What is the smallest action we could take that would have the biggest impact in that area?

7. What are some other ways of faithfully participating in political life that we haven't mentioned here?

8. When you consider your gifts, abilities, and life experiences, which of the aforementioned six options seems like the best fit for you?

9. What do you think should be your next steps? Spend some time praying for one another and encouraging one another about how to take action.

ACKNOWLEDGMENTS

It's hard to overstate how grateful I am for the congregation and leadership of Redemption Tempe. Your ability to stay at the table in the midst of political polarization has provided a glimpse of Jesus and displayed the fruit of the Spirit. I am especially grateful for Jim Mullins, my co-pastor and one of the wisest leaders I know, whom I had the honor of laboring alongside for years and whose genius is embedded in the best ideas and stories in these pages.

Words cannot express how grateful I am for Jenni Burke, my phenomenal agent and friend, and the whole publishing team at WaterBrook and Multnomah. A special shout-out to Laura Barker for providing direction on this project and Drew Dixon and Laura Wright for being such phenomenal editors.

I am sincerely grateful for the many friends who have read and provided feedback for portions of this book, especially Ben Adam, Beth Prochaska, Britney Wong, Carrie Vaughn, Chris St. John, Emma Tautolo, Jason Raber, Jim Campbell, Lance Brewer, Lily Hsueh, Michael Ly, Michel Duarte, Molly Yates, Rob Jones, Rob Wolfe, Tyler Hudgins, Tyler Wince, and the elders of Redemption Tempe. I'm also thankful to Eric and Amy Ludwig for providing space for writing retreats.

I want to thank Imago Dei Community, where I grew up in the faith for nearly two decades, who gave me a Christ-centered vision for civic engagement toward the good of the city and the flourishing of our neighbors. Thank you especially to Rick McKinley, whose leadership in the kingdom has left a legacy in my life, as it has in the lives of so many others.

Thank you to my family: my father, who's embodied sacrificial service and a commitment to public justice throughout my life; my mother, who's been a sign of Christ's expansive kingdom celebration that is welcoming to all; my brothers and extended family, who've always invited me to the party and embraced me wholeheartedly; and, of course, Holly, Aiden, James, and Jacob, the better party I'd always rather be at.

Thank you ultimately to Christ our King, who's welcomed me with open arms into the kingdom of his Father and the joy of his Spirit.

NOTES

Chapter 1: The Four Political Religions

1. The political theologian William Cavanaugh gives a provocative account of "religion"—from its ancient usage for social obligations (*religio*), which were as much civic, political, familial, and "secular" (to use an anachronistic term) as the things we consider "religious" today. The word is most likely etymologically derived from *religare*, meaning "to rebind" or "to bind fast" with a sense of piety or devotion. It has developed in modernity as a category used to describe a system of theological doctrine or belief and to marginalize certain forms of discourse from the public sphere. Yet, as Cavanaugh shows, it is a hard category to pin down and define, and modern politics is way more "religious" than many people think. See *The Myth of Religious Violence: Secular Ideology and the Roots of Modern Conflict* (New York: Oxford University Press, 2009), 57–122.

2. I'm following here in the steps of those like the philosopher James K. A. Smith, who draws out the liturgical nature of modern cultural life, with its various rhythms, rituals, and habits that form and shape us. See his three-volume Cultural Liturgies project, beginning with *Desiring the Kingdom: Worship, Worldview, and Cultural Formation* (Grand Rapids, Mich.: Baker Academic, 2009).

3. George Packer, "How America Fractured into Four Parts," *The Atlantic*, July/August 2021. This was later expanded into a book: *Last Best Hope: America in Crisis and Renewal* (New York: Picador, 2022).

4. Adapted from the back cover jacket of Packer, *Last Best Hope*.

5. I'm indebted to my friend and former co-pastor Jim Mullins for many of the core ideas in this chapter. They are used with permission.

6. This illustration is inspired by James K. A. Smith's description of the liturgy of the shopping mall in *Desiring the Kingdom*, chap. 3.

7. Ronald Reagan, quoted in Andrew Glass, "Reagan Delivers Farewell Address, Jan. 11, 1989," Politico, January 10, 2019, www.politico.com/story/2019/01/11/reagan-delivers-farewell -address-jan-11-1989-1088708.

8. The quote is from William McRaven, *Make Your Bed: Little Things That Can Change Your Life . . . and Maybe the World* (New York: Grand Central Publishing, 2017). Jordan Peterson famously unpacked the same idea on *The Ben Shapiro Show*, Sunday Special Episode 1 (YouTube, May 6, 2018), and in *12 Rules For Life: An Antidote to Chaos* (Toronto: Random House Canada, 2018), particularly Rule #6 ("Set your house in order before you criticize the world"), 147–60.

9. Jean-François Lyotard, quoted in "Jean-François Lyotard (1924– 1998)," Internet Encyclopedia of Philosophy, https://iep.utm .edu/lyotard.

10. Tom Nichols, *The Death of Expertise: The Campaign Against Established Knowledge and Why It Matters* (New York: Oxford University Press, 2017), back cover.

11. I'm grateful to Jim Mullins for this observation. Some of this chapter's conclusion is inspired by and adapted from content he's taught at Redemption Tempe; it's used with his permission.

Chapter 2: Pledging Allegiance to the King of Kings

1. Quoted in Richard Horsley, *Jesus and Empire: The Kingdom of God and the New World Disorder* (Minneapolis: Fortress, 2002), 23–24.

2. Philippians 2:9–11, ESV, using *confess* as an alternate rendering for the NIV's *acknowledge* (*exomologesetai*).

3. Matthew 28:18; Revelation 19:16.

4. Revelation 11:15, NKJV; see also Haggai 2:7; John 5:26–29; Acts 10:42; 2 Timothy 4:1; 1 Peter 4:5.

5. See Micah 6:8.

6. See Matthew 5:43–48; 16:24–26; 20:25–28; Romans 12:14–21.

7. See Psalms 2 and 110, the most quoted psalms in the New Testament.

8. Matthew W. Bates overplays his hand, in my opinion, yet still helpfully explores this theme in *Salvation by Allegiance Alone: Rethinking Faith, Works, and the Gospel of Jesus the King* (Grand Rapids, Mich.: Baker Academic, 2017). Although faith is characterized as receptive trust in the New Testament, it orders our lives toward obedience in union with Christ.

9. Matthew 20:25.

10. On Jesus's identification with Yahweh of the Old Testament, see Richard Bauckham's intertextual discussion of passages like Romans 10:13 (with Joel 2:32), Philippians 2:6–11 (with Isaiah 45:23; 52:13; and 53:12), and 1 Corinthians 8:5–6 (with Deuteronomy 4:35, 39; and 6:4), in *Jesus and the God of Israel: God Crucified and Other Studies on the New Testament's Christology of Divine Identity* (Grand Rapids, Mich.: Eerdmans, 2008), 182–232.

11. Psalm 47:2, 8.

12. See Genesis 2:15.

13. From Abraham Kuyper's sermon "Rooted and Grounded," in *On the Church: Collected Works in Public Theology* (Bellingham, Wash.: Lexham, 2016).

14. See Genesis 1:26–27; Revelation 7:9.

15. The philosopher Byung-Chul Han attributes much of this heightened anxiety to the replacement of a *disciplinary* society (which guides you in what you *should* do) with an *achievement* society (which encourages you to do whatever you *can* do). The resulting pressure to create an identity, to manufacture and present a "self" that justifies your existence, to be whoever you want to be in a way that achieves acceptance, value, and worth, is an enormous burden to bear. See *The Burnout Society* (Stanford, Calif.: Stanford University Press, 2015).

16. See Exodus 23:33; 2 Samuel 22:3; Psalm 18:1–6; Zechariah 2:5; Romans 16:20; Revelation 21:27.

17. Some of this "Ideology as Idolatry" section is adapted from content taught by Jim Mullins at Redemption Tempe; it's used with his permission.

18. Psalm 115:8.

19. See 1 Samuel 8:19–20.

20. See 1 Samuel 8:7.

21. Okay, that's a gross oversimplification of O'Donovan's thought. (He is one of my favorite political theologians!) His bigger emphasis is that God's reign above (sovereignty) and before (eschatology) puts pressure on politics, holding it accountable to a higher kingdom. Yet his account has immense explanatory power for the craziness we see today, when the confrontation and ordering that God's kingdom brings have been rejected and displaced. For a great inroad into O'Donovan's political theology (warning: it's academically thick!), see his *Desire of the Nations: Rediscovering the Roots of Political Theology* (New York: Cambridge University Press, 1999).

22. See Peter Beinart, "Breaking Faith: The Culture War over Religious Morality Has Faded; In Its Place Is Something Much Worse," *The Atlantic,* April 2017.

23. A paraphrase of Douthat's tweet from February 29, 2016, which included, "If you dislike the religious right, wait till you meet the post-religious right"; https://twitter.com/DouthatNYT/status/704462319074594816.

24. Friedrich Nietzsche, *Ecce Homo,* trans. R. J. Hollingdale (New York: Penguin Classics, 1992), https://genius.com/Friedrich-nietzsche-why-i-am-a-destiny-annotated.

25. Ephesians 6:12.

26. In Ephesians 6:12 quoted above, there is some question among interpreters as to the extent to which the powers in this passage are political versus spiritual, but I believe that a biblical worldview sees these realms as integrated. For example, in Luke 10:18, Jesus refers to seeing Satan (a spiritual power) "fall like lightning from heaven," yet the verse he's alluding to (Isaiah 14:12) refers to the king of Babylon (a political power). In Revelation, the apocalyptic symbol of the dragon is famously described as both Satan (a spiritual power) and the Roman Empire (a political power). Such examples assume that the spiritual and political are not isolated but intertwined.

27. Much of this "Come to the Table" section is adapted from content taught by Jim Mullins at Redemption Tempe; used with his permission.

28. See Isaiah 2:1–4; 55:1–2; Revelation 21:4–5; 19:7–10.
29. See Ephesians 6:12.

Chapter 3: Welcome to the King's Table

1. This is anecdotal—I haven't seen studies on this. But I've witnessed the trend in the Phoenix area and heard about it from other pastors across the country.
2. For those familiar with the "homogeneous unit" principle in the church-growth movement, this is the updated version: Security Steve is the new Saddleback Sam.
3. Thanks to my friend and former co-pastor Jim Mullins for this *leaning* versus *bowing* distinction.
4. See Luke 6:15; Acts 1:13.
5. See Matthew 9:9.
6. See Matthew 9:10; 11:19; 18:17; 21:31–32; Mark 2:15; Luke 5:30; 7:34; 18:9–14.
7. Luke 19:2; see verses 1–10.
8. See Matthew 5:43–48; 7:5; John 18:10–11; Romans 12:14–21. N. T. Wright gives a powerful defense of how central—and controversial—Jesus's call to forsake violent revolution was to his message, in *Jesus and the Victory of God* (Minneapolis: Fortress, 1996), 244–319.
9. See Matthew 6:19–24; Luke 12; 16; 19:1–10; 1 Timothy 6:10.
10. See Matthew 13:31–33; Mark 10:29–31.
11. See Matthew 4:18.
12. Colossians 4:14, ESV.
13. Luke's high education is evident in both the eloquent language of his writings and his frequent allusions to classical Greek authors. See Steve Reece, *The Formal Education of the Author of Luke–Acts* (London: T&T Clark, 2022), 29–50.
14. Although Paul wrote more books of the New Testament, the books of Luke and Acts (both authored by Luke) are the longest of the New Testament, accounting for more than 27.5 percent of its word count; see Ryan Nelson, "Who Was Saint Luke? The Beginner's Guide," Overviewbible.com, March 29, 2019, https://overviewbible.com/saint-luke.
15. Galatians 3:26, 28.

16. Thanks again to Jim Mullins for help developing these assessment questions.

Chapter 4: Ten Political Commandments

1. Exodus 20:2–3; Deuteronomy 5:6–7.
2. Luke 4:8, referring to Deuteronomy 6:13.
3. Joshua 5:13, MSG; see verse 14.
4. Jim Mullins, quoted in Troy Farah, "Here's What Happened at the Anti-Islam Protest and 'Draw Muhammad' Contest in Arizona," Vice News, May 30, 2015, www.vice.com/en/article/8x39mk/heres-what-happened-at-the-anti-islam-protest-and-draw-muhammad-contest-in-arizona.
5. Mark 12:31, quoting Leviticus 19:18.
6. See Luke 10:25–37.
7. John Calvin, *Institutes of the Christian Religion* (Philadelphia: Westminster, 1960), 695, http://thebriefing.com.au/2005/10/the-sum-of-the-christian-life-the-denial-of-ourselves.
8. Jim Mullins, personal correspondence with the author, January 10, 2023.
9. James 3:9.
10. James 3:9, ESV; see verse 10.
11. See James 3:11–12.
12. Vincent Bacote, *The Political Disciple: A Theology of Public Life* (Grand Rapids, Mich.: Zondervan, 2015), 42.
13. On the philosophical genealogy of expressive individualism and its ascendance as a driving story in the modern West, see Carl Trueman, *The Rise and Triumph of the Modern Self: Cultural Amnesia, Expressive Individualism, and the Road to Sexual Revolution* (Wheaton, Ill.: Crossway, 2020).
14. Eli Pariser introduced *filter bubble* to the lexicon and has some great anecdotes displaying the ways internet companies are skewing what we get, even on a Google search, and influencing our ability to get accurate news, in his *New York Times* bestseller *The Filter Bubble: How the New Personalized Web Is Changing What We Read and How We Think* (New York: Penguin, 2012).
15. Psalm 1:1–2, with *instruction* as an alternate rendering of *law*.
16. Some friends and I discuss these unhealthy versions in Re-

demption Tempe's podcast episode "Justice: Postmodern vs. Biblical Visions," *All of Life*, episode 9, March 25, 2021.

17. In the Old Testament, the Hebrew term *mishpat* occurs 421 times and *tsedaqah* 157 times. In the New Testament, the Greek term *dikaiosune* occurs 92 times and *krisis* 48 times.

18. Psalm 99:4, NLT; see also Psalm 106:3; Proverbs 21:3; Isaiah 1:17; Micah 6:8.

19. This is a popular paraphrase of Augustine's rebuke of Faustus in *Contra Faustum*, 17.3: "You ought to say plainly that you do not believe the gospel of Christ. For to believe what you please, and not to believe what you please, is to believe yourselves, and not the gospel."

20. A. J. Swoboda, *After Doubt: How to Question Your Faith Without Losing It* (Grand Rapids, Mich.: Brazos, 2021), 52–53.

21. Matthew 7:20, NASB, substituting *fruit* for the NIV's *fruits* to match the Galatians 5:22 reference. Some of this paragraph is adapted from my book *The Skeletons in God's Closet* (Nashville: Thomas Nelson, 2014), 198–99.

22. Galatians 5:22–23, ESV.

23. See Romans 12:21; 1 Peter 3:9.

24. Matthew 11:29, ESV.

25. Dane C. Ortlund, *Gentle and Lowly: The Heart of Christ for Sinners and Sufferers* (Wheaton, Ill.: Crossway, 2021), 19.

Chapter 5: Breakers, Fakers, and Makers

1. I'm grateful for Jim Mullins, my friend and former co-pastor, whose insights on peacemaking are threaded throughout this chapter; used with his permission.

2. See Judges 6:23–24; Isaiah 9:6–7; Romans 15:33; 16:20; 1 Corinthians 14:33; 2 Corinthians 13:11; Philippians 4:9; 1 Thessalonians 5:23; 2 Thessalonians 3:16; Hebrews 13:20–21.

3. Isaiah 9:6.

4. Ephesians 2:14.

5. Cornelius Plantinga, Jr., *Not the Way It's Supposed to Be: A Breviary of Sin* (Grand Rapids, Mich.: Eerdmans, 1999), 9–10.

6. Colossians 1:19–20 (emphasis added).

7. Matthew 5:9.

8. Acts 10:36, rendering *gospel* in place of *good news*, from *evange-*

lizomenos; 2 Corinthians 5:18–20; see also Jeremiah 29:7; Romans 5:1; Ephesians 2.

9. See John 20:21–22.

10. Matthew 7:4–5, ESV.

11. Matthew 18:15, ESV.

12. See Psalm 101:5; Proverbs 6:16–19; Matthew 12:36; Romans 1:29–30; Ephesians 4:29; 1 Timothy 5:13; Titus 3:2; James 1:26.

13. A helpful resource for assessing such situations is Darby Strickland, *Is It Abuse? A Biblical Guide to Identifying Domestic Abuse and Helping Victims* (Phillipsburg, N.J.: P&R, 2020).

14. See Matthew Soerens and Jenny Yang, *Welcoming the Stranger: Justice, Compassion, and Truth in the Immigration Debate* (Downers Grove, Ill.: InterVarsity, 2018).

15. James 1:19.

16. Although a refugee has never successfully executed an act of terrorism, there have been attempts.

17. Matthew 18:16, ESV.

18. Romans 5:8, 10, ESV.

19. Isaiah 53:5.

20. Romans 12:18.

21. See Luke 7:47.

22. Revelation 5:9, ESV.

Chapter 6: When to Be Bold

1. Larry Hurtado, *Destroyer of the Gods: Early Christian Distinctiveness in the Roman World* (Waco, Tex.: Baylor University Press, 2016). These five categories are my language, not Hurtado's, to highlight certain features from his work, adapted from similar language Tim Keller used in a talk at "The Gospel and Our Cities" conference in Chicago, Illinois (October 2018).

2. A paraphrase of part of the emperor Julian's letter to Arsacius.

3. 2 Corinthians 8:9.

4. See Rodney Stark, *The Rise of Christianity: How the Obscure, Marginal Jesus Movement Became the Dominant Religious Force in the Western World in a Few Centuries* (San Francisco, Calif.: HarperSanFrancisco, 1997), chaps. 2, 4, 7.

5. See Kyle Harper, *From Shame to Sin: The Christian Transforma-*

tion of Sexual Morality in Late Antiquity (Cambridge, Mass.: Harvard University Press, 2016).

6. See Stark, *Rise of Christianity,* chap. 5.

7. See Ephesians 5:21–6:9; Colossians 3:18–4:1. Larry Hurtado observes how countercultural and humanizing it was for women, children, and slaves to be addressed directly in such codes as persons with agency, in *Destroyer of the Gods,* 177–80. I gave a sermon on this called "The Revolution Starts at Home," June 15, 2022, www.tempe.redemptionaz.com/sermons/colossians.

8. See Stark, *Rise of Christianity,* chap. 5; Hurtado, *Destroyer of the Gods,* 145. Globally, the sex selection of females for abortion or infanticide, often referred to as gendercide, is still a tragic reality in our world today.

9. Hilarion's letter to his wife, Alis. "Papyrus Oxyrhynchus 744," in *Life in Egypt Under Roman Rule,* ed. Naphtali Lewis (New York: Oxford University Press, 1985), 54.

10. See Psalm 68:5–6; James 1:27.

11. From a talk Tim Keller gave at "The Gospel and Our Cities" conference in Chicago, Illinois (October 2018).

12. You can find information about the organizations at www .andcampaign.org and www.choosetruthovertribe.com.

13. See 2 Corinthians 5:11–21; Ephesians 1:3–10; 2:14–18; Colossians 1:15–20.

14. Isaiah 61:8, NLT.

15. Romans 12:15.

16. See 2 Corinthians 5:18–20.

17. "Redemption Church, Racism and the Gospel," available at https://bit.ly/3ZAoXWa.

18. "Justice: Postmodern vs. Biblical Visions," *All of Life* (podcast), episode 9, March 25, 2021.

19. See 1 Corinthians 12:21–26.

20. See Revelation 21–22.

21. Joshua Ryan Butler, *Beautiful Union: How God's Vision for Sex Points Us to the Good, Unlocks the True, and (Sort Of) Explains Everything* (Colorado Springs, Colo.: Multnomah, 2023).

22. This idea is inspired by and adapted from Russell Moore's call to "keep Christianity strange" in *Onward: Engaging the Culture Without Losing the Gospel* (Nashville: B&H, 2015).

23. See John 6:25–59.

24. John 6:60, ESV.

25. John 6:62, ESV.

26. John 6:66, ESV.

27. See Matthew 19:30; 20:26–28; 16:24–26; 1 Corinthians 1:18–31.

28. See Luke 2:7; 5:15–16, 29–31; 7:36–50; and 23:26–49.

29. John 6:68.

30. See Genesis 3.

31. See Revelation 19:11–21; inspired by and adapted from a line I heard Russell Moore give in a talk years ago, though I've been unable to locate the source.

32. Revelation 19:16.

Chapter 7: An Outpost of the Kingdom

1. For a great reflection on a spirituality for such everyday practices, see Tish Harrison Warren, *Liturgy of the Ordinary: Sacred Practices in Everyday Life* (Downers Grove, Ill.: InterVarsity, 2019).

2. Aleksandr Solzhenitsyn, *The Gulag Archipelago,* trans. Thomas P. Whitney (London: Vintage Classics, 2018).

3. See Luke 7:36–50, especially verse 47.

4. Luke 7:47.

5. Each element of our church's service is patterned on a movement in the biblical story: Creation, Fall, Redemption, and Restoration. The call to worship is loosely patterned on the Creation (It all starts with God). Confession aligns with the reality of the Fall (We've made a mess of things). The reading of God's Word, and its exposition in a sermon, then moves to Redemption (God's not done with us yet) before climaxing at the Lord's table in worship, which is all about restoration (Jesus is putting it all back together).

6. I love this part of the liturgy. As a preacher, it forces me to connect the message to Jesus, to tie our Scripture passage for the morning to the bigger picture of the gospel. (For what it's worth, I've never found a passage that didn't naturally lead to Jesus.) For our congregation, it encourages us to land not on "What a great message!" so much as "What a great Savior!"

7. Also Genesis 1, Noah's flood, and so on.

8. Paul Miller, *J-Curve: Dying and Rising with Jesus in Everyday Life* (Wheaton, Ill.: Crossway, 2019).
9. See John 6.
10. See Luke 22:7–23; 1 Corinthians 5:7.
11. See Matthew 4:4, referring to Deuteronomy 8:3; see also John 1:1–3, 14.
12. See Exodus 13:21.
13. Theologians like Stanley Hauerwas have called the church a "colony of the kingdom." Although colonization can have negative associations today, the idea is a group of people, living together in a foreign land, whose ultimate allegiance is to another kingdom. Similarly, God's kingdom is invading the powers of this world, subversively planting churches like colonies beneath their reign. The church's allegiance is to an upside-down kingdom (at least it's supposed to be!) where these colonies are marked not by power grabs and exploitation but rather by sacrificial service and enemy love.

Chapter 8: Formational Practices for a Polarized World

1. I'm grateful for Jim Mullins, my friend and former co-pastor, whose insights are threaded throughout this chapter; used with his permission.
2. See Brett McCracken, *The Wisdom Pyramid: Feeding Your Soul in a Post-Truth World* (Wheaton, Ill.: Crossway, 2021).
3. Joe Biden, quoted in Cara Bentley, "Biden Quotes Isaiah, 'Here I Am Lord, Send Me,' Referencing US Military's Desire to Go to Afghanistan," Premiere Christian News, August 27, 2021, https://premierchristian.news/en/news/article/biden-quotes -isaiah-here-i-am-lord-send-me-referencing-us-military-s -desire-to-go-to-afghanistan.
4. Matthew 26:11; Mark 14:7; see also John 12:8.
5. Moreover, the story surrounding Jesus's statement is about a lower-class woman generously pouring out her best on Jesus while being critiqued by wealthy onlookers. John 12:6 makes clear that the motive in their critique of her was greed, which Jesus was confronting with this response.
6. Matthew 7:1.
7. See 1 Corinthians 5, for example, where we're called as the

church not to judge the world but to judge one another, helping one another to pursue holiness together.

8. Donald Trump, quoted in Nolan D. McCaskill, "Trump's Favorite Bible Verse: 'Eye for an Eye,'" Politico, April 14, 2016, www.politico.com/blogs/2016-gop-primary-live-updates-and-results/2016/04/trump-favorite-bible-verse-221954.

9. See Matthew 5:38–48; Romans 12:14–21.

10. Craig G. Bartholomew and Michael W. Goheen, *The Drama of Scripture: Finding Our Place in the Biblical Story* (London: SPCK, 2017), 12.

11. Check out some great reading plans at BibleProject (www.bibleproject.com), She Reads Truth (www.shereadstruth.com), and He Reads Truth (www.hereadstruth.com).

12. See Bill Bishop and Robert G. Cushing, *The Big Sort: Why the Clustering of Like-Minded America Is Tearing Us Apart* (Boston: Mariner Books, 2009).

13. Bishop and Cushing, *Big Sort*, 68.

14. 1 Timothy 2:2.

15. 1 Timothy 2:1.

16. Matthew 6:10.

Chapter 9: Creative Options for Political Involvement

1. Thank you to Jim Mullins, my friend and former co-pastor, who helped develop these six options together.

2. Oxford English Dictionary, s.v. "subsidiarity," 2019.

3. See Linda Valdez, "Valdez: Why Pastors Oppose Predatory Lending," *AZ Central*, April 13, 2016, www.azcentral.com/story/opinion/op-ed/lindavaldez/2016/04/13/valdez-why-pastors-oppose-predatory-lending/83010922.

4. See Daniel 1; shout-out to Rick McKinley, from Imago Dei Community, whom I heard make this observation years ago.

5. Abraham Kuyper, *Lectures on Calvinism* (Peabody, Mass.: Hendrickson, 2008), viii.

6. Martin Luther King, Jr., "Letter from Birmingham Jail," April 16, 1963.

7. See Daniel 6:10.

8. Steven Garber, *Visions of Vocation: Common Grace for the Common Good* (Downers Grove, Ill.: InterVarsity, 2014), 55.

9. George Eliot, *Middlemarch* (New York: Caldwell), chap. 86, Project Gutenberg, www.gutenberg.org.

10. John Henry Newman, *Historical Sketches*, vol. 3, *Rise and Progress of Universities; Northmen and Normans in England and Ireland; Medieval Oxford; Convocation of Canterbury* (London: Longmans, Green, 1970), 398.

11. David J. Bosch, *Transforming Mission: Paradigm Shifts in Theology and Mission* (Maryknoll, N.Y.: Orbis, 2011), 237.

12. An influential and classic work from this perspective is Stanley Hauerwas and William Willimon, *Resident Aliens: Life in the Christian Colony* (Nashville: Abingdon, 1989).

13. You can learn more about ranked-choice voting at https://ballotpedia.org/Ranked-choice_voting_(RCV).

14. Shout-out to Jim Mullins for this helpful illustration.

15. If a candidate wins a majority of first-preference votes, that candidate wins the election. If they don't win a majority, you begin to count second- and third-preference votes, and so on, until there's a candidate who wins the majority.

Conclusion

1. Matthew 9:10.

Joshua Ryan Butler is a pastor and the author of *Beautiful Union, The Skeletons in God's Closet,* and *The Pursuing God.* He loves shifting paradigms to help people who wrestle with tough topics of the Christian faith. Josh and his family—his wife, Holly; his daughter, Aiden; and his sons, James and Jacob—enjoy spending time with friends over great meals and exploring the scenic beauty of God's creation.